Living with a WILLY

Nick Fisher has been a freelance journalist for ten years, working for a wide variety of teenage and women's magazines and news-papers. He was the resident agony uncle for *Just Seventeen* and also writes scripts for television and radio. He is a mad-keen angler and collects American cars. He currently lives in east London with his wife Helen and whippet Ollie.

Also by Nick Fisher

Boys About Boys
The facts, fears and fantasies

Living
with a
WILLY

Nick Fisher

MACMILLAN CHILDREN'S
BOOKS

THE INSIDE STORY

First published 1994 by Pan Macmillan Children's Books
This edition reprinted 1995 by Macmillan Children's Books
a division of Macmillan Publishers Limited
20 New Wharf Road, London N1 9RR
Basingstoke and Oxford
Associated companies throughout the world
www.panmacmillan.com

ISBN 978-0-330-33248-4

23 25 27 29 28 26 24

A CIP catalogue record for this book is available from
the British Library.

Typeset by Intype Libra Ltd
Printed and bound in the UK by
CPI Mackays, Chatham ME5 8TD

Contents

5 Sex & your Sausage

6 Any Other Business

7 Living with your Willy

The Winkle Years

Growing up with a willy nestling down your Y-fronts is a strange business. Some days it's a major hoot. Other days it's a prime source of serious depression.

The early years are no problem – so long as you quickly gain a firm respect for zip fasteners. Your mum calls it your 'winkle', your granny sometimes points it for you when you have a 'tinkle' in the toilet round her house, and everyone thinks that you and it are really very cute. Sometimes when you're out shopping with your mum, or down at the beach, or even perched on the hard shoulder of a motorway and you get caught short, your mum'll just drop your pants, aim the winkle and you get to wee where you stand.

And if passers-by see you having a wee-wee, even catch a glimpse of your tiny tackle, they just smile warmly and nudge each other. The sight of a tousle-haired tot with his tiny trousers round his ankles is a cute, funny, characterful scene. In fact it's thought to be so cute you can even buy naff little china figures of small lads taking a leak.

But, fifteen years later on, you try it again; you get your knob out for a slash down the shopping precinct and you'll find yourself in bigger trouble than you ever dreamed. No sooner have you pointed Percy than the police'll pounce on you, arrest you, throw you in the nick and charge you with indecent exposure. You'll be labelled a monster and hated by society at large. But it's the same winkle. Same function. Society just doesn't see it the same way.

Suddenly, your funny sausage has become a dirty, evil symbol of sex and depravity. It's a strange business.

The first few years of living with a willy are a great laugh. You can prod it with your Lego blocks and it looks all squidgy and feels funny. As you get bigger you can use it to write your name in yellow wee on the crisp white snow. You can show it to your friends and have competitions to see who can pee the highest up the wall.

But then it all starts to get complicated. Puberty comes along and the cheeky little chipolata starts to get a bit bigger and hair starts to grow round it – although neither the hair nor the size happen fast enough or big enough.

Instead of showing it to all your mates and using it to put out bonfires, suddenly you get all coy and serious about it. You don't let your mum see it any more. If your gran tried to point it for you, you'd die. And having showers at school after games becomes a big ordeal because, instead of all your mates having identical trouser tackle, they've each started to develop at alarmingly different rates.

Some lads seem to have huge hefty members as fat as your arm surrounded by great tufts of thick curly hair, while others still have the pink winkle and bum-fluff kit. Nature can be very cruel.

All of a sudden the thing that gave you so many rib-tickling childish laughs weeing up the back of the Portakabin at school is causing you a lot of grief. It's making you embarrassed about its dimensions and developmental progress. It's causing you to sleep badly and worry about your normality.

And then, if all that's not enough, it starts to lead a life of its own. When you reach puberty, 'Stiffy' might as well be your middle name. You only have to sneeze and you get an erection. Even flossing your teeth can cause a major bulge in the boxers. You sit on a bus – you get a hard on. You watch telly – you get a hard on. You think of girls – you get a hard on. You think of *Geography* – you get a hard on. There is no rhyme or reason to it. Anything can give you a stiffy.

Rather than being proud and pleased that the tackle all performs correctly, if a little too frequently, instead you get paranoid. What if someone sees your bulge? What if they realize you've got a hard on? The prospect seems totally horrifying. It feels as if without a shadow of a doubt, having your unwanted erection noticed would signify the end of the world as we know it. You would be a social outcast until you die. You'd be headline news in several national newspapers. SCHOOLBOY GETS STIFFY. Shock horror probe. BBC2 would probably make documentaries about you.

Well, they *wouldn't*. But that's what it *feels* like.

And no one understands. Girls don't understand. To you it seems their puberty worries are totally the other way round. They're only concerned with things not showing *enough*. They want their breasts to be larger and more prominent. You might want a bigger knob, but you certainly don't want it to show more.

The whole shame and taboo stuff that's begun to form around your penis and its unpredictable ways means you don't talk about it. You keep it secret, and so it worries you even more. But then *who* would you talk about it to? Your mates will only laugh and then use your fears and confessions as ammunition for taking the mickey at a later date. Your mum wouldn't understand and your dad's not easy to talk to. So you just worry in silence.

After puberty's had its wicked way, then adulthood and Performance Fear grabs you by the balls. Although, legally, you're adult enough to have sex at sixteen, you may well feel that you're not yet ready to share your willy for a while longer. When you get to being an adult, gone are those days of childish fun and yellow snow. Now you're reading magazine articles about sex technique and 'giving your partner multiple orgasms'. The winkle that was there just for your very own amusement and entertainment has developed into this highly complicated sex tool. And, let's face it, inviting along a third party to join you and your willy in the fun is a big step to take.

You're supposed to know just how to use it to give maximum pleasure to the wife or girlfriend. And if you don't, then you're not a 'real man'. So now you've got a whole heap of new worries. It's not just: 'When's it going to go stiff?' 'Will anyone see it?' and 'Is it big enough to hold its own in the communal showers?' – now it's: 'Do I know how to use it properly?' 'Will it perform as it's meant to?' and 'Will she be sexually satisfied?'

Living with a willy is not easy. It's a funny little stump, stuck in the most impractical place and built to a completely nutty design. When it's cold it feels like a whelk sitting on two dried prunes, and when it's warm it's like a limp boiled crab-stick leaning against a pair of eggs in a velvet pouch.

Love it or hate it, you're stuck with it. There's nothing you can do to change it, exchange it, modify or improve it. All you can really hope to do is try and learn to love it.

Willy Worries

2

Is it *big* enough?

The Number One worry when it comes to the willy is size. Of all the problem letters I've received for the agony columns I write, fears about having a penis which is too small outweigh other fears by about twenty to one. Men and boys of all ages are convinced that their dicks are too small.

Usually, what they think this means is that they'll be ridiculed by their mates, rejected by women and generally destined to a life of loneliness and sorrow. It's amazing how much importance can be attached to such a silly tuft of flesh.

But the truth is, boys do worry themselves into a right old state over their vital statistics. Some get anxious when they find out what other boys have got:

● When I'm in the changing room at school, I'm constantly looking at other boys' penises. I look because mine is relatively small and I think other boys' penises are larger than mine.

Dave (13)

● I have measured my penis a number of times with a ruler and I compared it with the average statistics. I am fifteen, but my penis only falls into the average category for twelve-year-olds. I don't want to have sex yet but I'm getting very worried that I won't be able to when I get older.

Mark

A lot of penis anxiety can be generated in the privacy of your own bedroom with a clear plastic ruler and a screwed-up impression of how long you think the 'average' penis size is supposed to be. In fact, measuring your willy has got to be one of the easiest ways of worrying and depressing yourself. Of course, though, matching up to someone else can be even worse:

● I am a twelve-year-old who is afraid of being abnormal. My friend can get an erection without doing anything. We also measured each other's penises and his is 2cm bigger than mine. I want to know if I have a problem. I'm too embarrassed to go to a doctor or ask my mum.

Tony

● I am seventeen. My penis is only 8cm long. My friends' penises all look bigger than mine. One night when I was at a friend's house his diary was open and I noticed he had written the length of his penis every month. His penis is 14cm long. Is there something wrong with me?

Greg

Rather than just having their own private concerns, some boys seem to take delight in fuelling and feeding each other's fears. The way they do this is by making each other feel desperately insecure about the size of their tackle. This might be a clever sort of diversionary tactic. If you can make someone else worried sick about their trouser stick, then maybe you don't have to worry so much about your own. Certainly the old bullying tactic of picking on someone and making fun of their willy means others follow suit. That way you can create a focus for their cruel attentions. A focus that definitely isn't on your own crown jewels.

● I'm thirteen years old. I have a small penis and no pubic hair, but all my friends have. When we have showers I am the only one who keeps my pants on, so they call me 'Maggot' and they tell all the girls. So now I have no friends. I am so depressed I want to kill myself.

Matthew

● I am fifteen and I have am embarrassing problem: my penis is too small and I have no pubic hair. Even my so-called friends laugh at me when I'm in the showers after PE. Sometimes I wonder if life is worth living.

Colin

● I am a wimp with a 5 inch willy. I get teased and stripped in class and PE. The teacher knows but doesn't do anything to help. You are my last resort.

Very depressed

● I'm thirteen and I get teased a lot because
my penis is very small. When my class
has showers after PE, everyone notices and
points and teases me. Now all the girls in my
class know as well.

Alex

It's obviously a pretty horrible experience being teased
by your mates about the supposedly small size of your
penis. For some boys it feels so bad they think life's
not worth living. But what's seen to be even worse is
when girls get to know about it too.

One big worry is that your mates will take the
mickey about your penis so much that the girls find
out and they then laugh at you as well. And strangely
enough it works the opposite way round too, where
you worry that the girls will find out first and then
tell all your mates:

● I'm a nineteen-year-old man and my penis
is only 4½ cm big. I get really embarrassed
when my friends boast about how big their
penises are as mine is only small. When they
ask me how big mine is I lie. I have been asked
to have sexual intercourse by my girlfriend.
But I'm too frightened to have sex in case she
laughs and tells everyone about my penis.

Depressed

In fact, girls seem to get blamed a lot for making boys
feel embarrassed and insecure about their tackle. The
two main accusations come from boys who have been
rejected by girls because they've got what they think
is a weenie willy, and those who assume they *will* be
rejected if she finds out their equipment's not up to
scratch.

Some boys claim to have *already* been rejected:

● I am a nineteen-year-old student on the verge of suicide due to an extremely embarrassing problem which is the very slow growth of my penis. I have been recently dumped by my girlfriend due to the fact that I was a total flop in bed. When I measured it last, it was 3½ inches maximum.

Anon

● I am eighteen and had a major setback recently. I met this girl on holiday in Corfu. Everything went well until the last night when she asked me to have sex with her. When we stripped and she saw my penis, she laughed out loud and then went back to her room. I felt rejected because my penis isn't up to standard.

James

● I am seventeen and I had a sixteen-year-old girlfriend until I had sex with her. We told each other how much we loved each other and decided to go for it. The day after she finished with me, she began to call me Pee Wee and told everyone I had a small penis.

Distressed

● I am sixteen. I first found out I had a problem when a girl I'd been going out with for three years offered to sleep with me. When I undressed she took one look at me and laughed. She refused to have sex with me. Then shortly after she ended our relationship and told the whole school.

Anon

Most of the letters are about a *fear* of being rejected for being too small. It's the minority of boys who claim to have already been rejected. Most claim to be too scared to make any advances or follow through to the sex part in relationships because they're so sure they *will* be rejected:

● I am sixteen and still a virgin. I'm the only virgin in my class. The reason for this is my penis is relatively small. I have had the chance to lose my virginity twice but am far too embarrassed about my penis.

Tom

● I'm very worried about the size of my manhood. I'm thirteen and going out with a girl who wants to begin touching me but I'm scared she will dump me when she sees the size of my penis. I know she has been out with boys of sixteen, so they will have been bigger than me. Are there any tablets I can get to improve my size?

Michael

● I've got a steady girlfriend and we're ready to sleep together (we are both sixteen). We have thought about it very carefully and decided it's the right thing to do. The only thing is that we have never seen each other naked before and my penis is not all that big. I'm worried that when she sees my penis she won't want to make love with me any more.

Anon

Girls get blamed for making boys scared about not measuring up to their expectations. But the paranoia of penis size is so strong that some boys need very little encouragement to feel worried. In fact, they don't need to have been told anything by girls, they can feel scared all on their own:

I am seventeen. For the last year my penis doesn't seem to be getting any larger. Although I put myself around with girls, they don't say anything to my face, but I'm sure they do have a laugh at me in the local pub.

Danny

I'm sixteen, my penis has not grown to the size I expected. I'm worried about going out with girls in case I get around to sexual contact and they find out about my problem and I would become the laughing stock of the town.

Alan

Even things like television programmes designed to put people's minds at rest can have the opposite effect on a boy, if there's already a seed of doubt sown in his head about his dimensions:

My worry is concerned with condoms. My fear is that when I try to put one on it will slip off. I am fifteen and when fully erect my penis measures 5½ inches from top to bottom. I worry about this all the time and my worry was intensified after watching a programme on AIDS, which showed a condom being put on an enormous model penis.

Anon

The whole issue about penis size seems to be directly connected with self esteem. The notion is that if a boy's got a big willy then he can feel big about himself. But if he thinks he's got a small one then he'll feel ashamed, inadequate and inferior. And it's all connected to his status and reputation amongst his peer group too. Having a tiny dick gets regarded as just about the worst thing imaginable. The fear is that a minute member will get you laughed at by your mates and rejected by women.

It seems truly bizarre that such a small organ can have such a monumental effect. No other part of a boy's body is steeped in such importance. Not even the human brain, the biggest, most incredible, most complex, most evolved organ on the face of this earth, the very thing that controls and kicks off every single move we take and thought we make. The brain doesn't get a fraction of the worry spent on it that the simple floppy flap that dangles between a boy's thighs does.

In all the letters I've answered from boys, I must have had a couple of thousand just on the fear of having a small penis. But I can't remember receiving even one single letter worrying about having an undersized brain or not enough IQ.

Girls' view of the willy

As so many boys seem to get in a major tizz about the size of their todger and what girls' reactions to it will be, it seems only fair to let the girls have their say. After publishing one letter from a boy who was deeply depressed about his dimensions, I encouraged girls to write in and explain what they feel about boys who think they're lacking in the trouser department:

◆ We are three sixteen-year-old girls who all think this is a silly thing to worry about. We hope we speak for the majority of girls when we say it doesn't matter about penis size. All of us would rather go with a bloke who didn't brag about having a large penis.

Ravers from Poole

◆ I had to laugh because I really do not think anyone is that bothered. Other girls only laugh about the names boys get called because they think it's good to have a laugh. The boys only pick on you because it makes them look big, mature lads. But they are only insecure about themselves. Myself, I am not bothered one little bit what size it is.

Annie (16)

◆ If you're looking for a decent girlfriend she won't care what size your penis is, as it's the person inside that she'll be interested in. I hate it when boys go around bragging about the size of their penis. It seems they want to attract attention to themselves and they only have one thing on their minds anyway. If everyone had the same-sized everything, life would be boring.

Cathy (16)

◆ When I go out with boys, the size of their penis makes no difference at all. Sex is a private affair of love and trust. Not all girls worry about that sort of thing. I love a boy for him, not the size of his penis.

Sally

◆ I'm a sixteen-year-old girl and personally I think the size of a boy's penis doesn't matter. As long as you get on well and love each other, things like that shouldn't matter. If girls do laugh at you, they're just being immature and not worth bothering about.

Claire

◆ If your girlfriend really loves you, the last thing she'll be worrying about is the size of your penis.

Beverley (17)

None of the girls who wrote said that the boy who thought his penis was very small should be ashamed. None said that he was unacceptable, unlovable and unworthy to call himself male. Quite the opposite, all of them told him it didn't matter, wasn't an issue and that the boys who took the michael were just immature tossers.

It's all so confusing. On the one hand some of your mates are suggesting that any boy who doesn't measure up is a 'Maggot', 'Weenie' or 'Baby Bio'. Yet the girls are telling you it's no big deal, doesn't matter, there's more to you than your knob and that, at the end of the day, personality is more important than prick.

So why does worry about your willy size cut so deep?

Maybe it's made worse by the fact that in your teens you haven't developed your personality that much, you haven't built a lot of self confidence or discovered your attractive hidden depths. So everything is judged on a fairly superficial level.

It's as though you're not aware of how much there is of you *inside*, so you simply compare and compete

with what's on the *outside*. You don't yet understand and appreciate the breadth of your individuality, so instead you just get obsessed about the length of your dick.

It's easily done – but ultimately pointless.

A few *truths* about your todger

Size doesn't matter

Even if you had a knob 12 inches long, as thick as your wrist and as stout as a truncheon, it wouldn't make you a better lover, a better man or a more attractive date. You could be hung like a donkey, but still be an insensitive, unsensual and selfish lover.

It's not quantity that matters, it's quality. The quality of the personality – not the prick.

The truth is, when push comes to shove, most knobs don't vary that much anyway. If you glanced around a crowded changing room to check out the array of knobs (and most boys *do*, not because of any homosexual tendencies, purely as a matter of curiosity), you'd think that they came in all shapes and sizes. And they do when they're limp. But erect, they all roughly even out.

Limp they are easily affected by temperature. In a hot steamy room, most dicks will dangle and droop nicely, but catch them in a draught of cold air or dip them in a swimming pool and they'll soon shrivel up like a mummified whelk. Every lad has experienced the sensation of climbing out of a chilly pool and feeling like your nuts are rapidly retreating back inside your body like a tortoise into his shell.

Nervous situations don't exactly promote the profile of your penis either. A good dose of fear soon sends your tackle into fold-away mode. It's probably some clever trick of Mother Nature, done to protect your equipment in moments of danger. Like if some marauding bear was attacking you, your dick would instantly shrink to the size of a baked bean so that Mr Bear couldn't purposely rip it off. No doubt it's a useful ability when you're off fending for yourself in the Great Outdoors. But it's a real drag at penis parade time down at the changing rooms when you get to feeling a tad nervous.

Some teenage boys do spend a fair amount of time looking at each other's penises in changing rooms or similar situations and often they'll have a laugh and a comment at someone else's expense.

When you get older, the laughing and the pointing stops. In fact grown men try very hard not to be seen looking at other men's penises. The main fear is that they don't want to be thought of as being gay. But they still want to look. We *all* do. So, they do it surreptitiously and just try to catch a quick glance. It's human nature. It's not that we want to ogle and stare, far from it. We just want a peek, just to check what each other is packing.

It's all just an optical illusion

In a lifetime most men see more penises than women ever do. But there's something very strange about looking at other blokes' dicks. It's something to do with perspective and foreshortening. Other blokes' knobs always look bigger than your own. If you look down at your todger then take a glance across at someone else's, it always seems like they've got more to show.

But, if you've ever had a pee in the toilet of one of those posh InterCity trains, you'll know that it's all just a trick of the light. The thing is that posh trains have mirrors mounted behind the toilets, so you can watch your knob as you take a leak. The effect is startling. Suddenly, you're seeing it as others see it, and the amazing thing is, it looks much better and bigger than it does from above!

We're all playing with the same bat

The whole thing is nonsense though, because penises just don't vary in size that much. When they're limp, most penises measure somewhere between 2 inches and 4½ inches. And when they're erect they normally vary between 5 inches and 7 inches, with the average adult penis being about 6 inches when fully erect. So at the very most we're talking about a couple of inches' variation, which is no big deal. Especially as the size of the penis doesn't make any difference to the way it performs.

Generally, smaller penises will increase in size more as they grow erect than larger penises, which may just stiffen rather than expand. And it makes little or no difference inside a woman, as her vagina can shape itself to fit any size of penis.

So what if your penis *does* fall into the smaller end of the scale? If it really worries you and you feel the need to do something about it, then the best thing is to learn to be a caring lover. Learn about foreplay, learn how to massage, learn how to give long lingering kisses and have a sensual touch.

Because, at the end of the day, if you're worried about how you rate as a lover, it's not your penis you want to be considering. As a rule most women don't get the most sexual satisfaction out of a man's penis. Most women find it much easier to reach an orgasm by having their clitoris touched and stroked than by being prodded by a willy, no matter what its size.

Small willies can be just as effective or ineffective as big willies. It's not the small piece of flesh in your trousers that matters so much as the big piece of flesh that's attached to it.

Success with sex and women is not down to what you've got in your pants, it's what you've got in your head that really counts.

A few *lies* about the willy

1 'If you've got big ears you've got a big dick.'

2 'Big feet are a sure indication of a big dick.'

3 'Large thumbs mean long length.'

4 'If a girl gives you a hard on and doesn't make you come your balls will explode or turn blue.'

5 'Black guys have bigger dongs.'

6 'The bigger your prick the more manly you are.'

7 'The fatter your flapper the more fertile you are.'

8 'The longer your length the more sex you get.'

9 'Women like sex better with well-hung men.'

10 'Too much masturbation can make you infertile.'

11 'Wanking makes you blind.'

12 'Rubbing it too often can wear it down.'

All of the above statements are total and absolute tosh.

No other part of the male anatomy causes such a stir or has had so much myth cloaked around it. An awful lot of rubbish gets talked about knobs. Maybe it's just a ploy to keep them interesting. The problem is that you don't get given an instruction manual when you grow a willy. So you have to rely on information from other willy users, who often haven't quite worked out what's what themselves. But instead of copping to the fact that they don't really know either, they make up some tale to cover themselves.

So what happens is that, round the back of the Portakabin at school, we all hear an awful lot of nonsense and often go on believing it for years to come.

A willy too big to be *true*

If you think about the slang used to describe an adult willy it all has a certain weighty substance to it: words like beef, dong, whanger, rod, bazooka, meat and truncheon all suggest size and solidity. Maybe this preference for big-sounding descriptions relates directly to the enormous number of men who are worried that their penis is too small. Maybe it's a sort of language compensation exercise. If a man's worried that he's got a bit of a weenie willy, but insists on calling it his 'chopper', he might possibly get to feel a little better. Who knows?

Big dicks are as rare as little pricks. Very few people have penises outside the average 5–7-inch size band. And only a minute percentage of the male population has anything touching on 9 inches or over. But still the legend of the big cock lives on. There's a million and one jokes and sayings that we all grow up hearing. Stuff like: I knew this girl who said she'd never go out with a bloke who didn't have 12 inches – so I had to tell her, I'm sorry, love, but I'm not having 3 inches chopped off for anyone.

Or the one that goes: I got asked to a fancy dress party last night but I didn't have anything to wear –

so I just slung my cock over my shoulder and went as a petrol pump.

Then there's T-shirts and Y-fronts with slogans like: I've got 12 inches but I don't use it as a rule.

There's a whole mythology built up around men with big willies. It's seen as a symbol of potency and power and masculinity. Which of course means big cocks are also objects of envy and fantasy.

Teenage boys and even grown men often fantasize about having enormous equipment. Some even feel the need to write letters about it:

I have a very bad problem. Whenever we have to shower after PE at school I always have to make excuses as I'm too embarrassed to shower with the other boys. This is because I have a very large penis. It is twice as big as some of my friends'. Why do I have such a large penis and will it affect my sex life? I might be too big to fit in the girl. I'm only twelve, so what will I be like when I'm older!

Worried big boy

Every time I have a shower after a match all the lads continually pick on me because I have a very large penis. It is roughly 11 inches long! Is this normal? I don't want to confront my mum because she would want me to show her. I am very embarrassed because some girls laugh at the huge bulge in my trousers. One girl keeps asking me out. Is she just after sex or does she genuinely like me?

Anon

● I am a thirteen-year-old boy. My problem is the opposite to the letters you get from boys my age. My penis is too large. I am treated as an outcast because of this and no boys like me because girls find me so attractive. Showers after PE are always very embarrassing. Is there any way I can make it smaller?

Concerned

All the 'big' boys' fantasies seem to have the same element, which includes being seen in the showers by all their mates. And although in their fantasy it might be described as 'embarrassing' to be seen with such a big penis, the general feeling is that they want other boys to be jealous of their tackle. And of course there's still the notion that having a big dick means that girls will automatically find you irresistible.

Another common situation is when boys have lied and kidded about their dimensions to all their mates, but somewhere along the line the plan has backfired:

● At school I am always boasting that I have the biggest penis and I never went in the showers after games, so no one knows any different. Then one day my PE teacher forced me to go into the shower because I was so muddy. Everyone started looking at me and taking the mickey. Now I cannot take much more. I may top myself.

Steven (13)

● I am an upset fourteen-year-old. Rumours have been going round school that I have a large penis and it has helped increase my sex life. But the other day in PE two girls looked down the leg of my shorts and announced that I had actually got a small penis. Now that everyone knows the first rumours were a lie I am being made fun of and sniggered at by classmates.

Concerned of Derbyshire

The sad thing is that any boys who genuinely do have bigger than average penises don't actually think that girls are going to queue up to have sex with them, quite the opposite. The most common fear is that having a large penis will make you unacceptable sexually and unlovable. The worry is that having an abnormally large penis will mean you'll get rejected for being a freak.

In reality though, the vagina is an incredible sex organ which is able to contract and expand. The opening to the vagina is a ring of muscle which is usually small and tight but which can *relax* enough and expand to allow a baby's head and body to pass through. So, the chances of a penis ever being too big to fit inside simply don't exist. Just remember about the relaxing bit.

So, no matter how big or small or achingly average your willy, wand, thing, string or dingaling is, it *will* work. It will fit. It will basically be just about the same as everyone else's.

But most of all it will still only be a small part of the *whole* you. It's not your be-all and end-all. It's not who you are or what you do. It's just the same silly sausage you used to write your name with in the snow. The trick is just not to take it too seriously.

Tackle Trouble

3

(when things don't seem right in the trouser department)

Bendy ones

Considering that so much laddish talk and smutty literature refers to willies that are 'ramrod erections' or 'steel-straight throbbing lengths of manhood', it might come as a bit of a surprise to learn that most erections are far from straight.

Nearly all of them tend to have a curvy bend upwards and a great many also have a bit of a bend or a lean to either side. Bendy ones are perfectly normal and make absolutely no difference to sex, weeing, wanking or using it as a thing to drown plastic ducks in the bath.

Not every boy knows how normal a bend can be. Bends only show up when the penis is erect. And although most men see far more penises in a lifetime than most women do, the thing heterosexual blokes practically never see is another *erect* penis. Sure, you get to see several limp ones in changing rooms and showers. But an erect one is a whole different kettle of fish. By not seeing other erections, men don't know what a strange range of shapes and angles can quite naturally occur.

And as with so many of these things, not knowing and not talking about it leads to worrying:

● I'm fifteen and I've never been out with a girl. All my friends have had several sexual relationships and they are beginning to think that I am gay as I appear not to be interested in girls. But the problem is that I'm worried if I go with a girl she will find out about the bend in my penis. I'm very self-conscious about this and worried that I'll never be capable of a sexual relationship.

Nathan

● I'm sixteen and I've been going with this girl for a while. It began to get heavy; she's started to drop hints about having sex. I'm not scared, but it's just that I've been masturbating quite frequently for a couple of years now and my penis has got a slight lean to it. It curves to the left when erect. I just want to know if it will affect or interfere with my sex life in any way? I also want to know if I'm the only one who is like this or not.

Anxious

Boys worry that having a bendy penis will make them sexually unacceptable or sexually incompatible. They also worry that they're a freak and their mates'll find out and tease them. And some even worry that they've done something wrong and caused their penis to curve in a weird way. Usually they think they've done this by too much masturbating; they tend to feel a little bit guilty about that anyway (see p. 55).

But bends and curves are not a problem. As long as everything functions properly there's nothing to

worry about. And even a very leaning or bendy penis won't feel any different to a girl during sex.

A bend too far

There is a very rare medical condition that can affect the penis which is called Peyronie's disease, named after the French doctor who discovered it two hundred years ago. This is when the curvature of the penis is very severe and also painful when erect. The condition makes intercourse impossible, not because of the bend, but because of the real pain that comes with erection.

No one knows why Peyronie's disease occurs, but what happens is that the tissue inside the penis, which is usually spongy, gets covered in scar tissue which stops it from expanding uniformly.

Thankfully it's an extremely rare condition, and one which can sometimes be corrected with skin grafts and surgery.

Circum*cis*ion

The most common surgery to be performed on the willy is circumcision. Usually it's done to boy babies either for religious, hygienic or cultural reasons and is only normally done to teenage or adult penises for health reasons.

Circumcision is a fairly simple operation to remove the foreskin. Jews, Muslims, Coptic Christians and many African tribes perform circumcisions on their young or baby boys. In the Jewish religion baby boys are ritually circumcised when they reach the age of eight days.

Some historians believe that circumcision began amongst the tribes of West Africa, who lopped off their foreskins, not for any health or religious reasons, but as a way of marking members of their tribe – literally!

In America circumcision has become a fashion. Up to one and a half million circumcisions are carried out every year for no reason other than that some people believe it's better without than with. In a way, you could say that's a weird sort of tribal recognition thing too.

In the days of the ancient Greeks, the shiny head of the penis (the glans) was considered to be sacred. To expose it was seen as very rude and shocking. Yet all the Olympic athletes competed in the nude. So to avoid any embarrassment and unwanted flashing they would tie the foreskin closed with a bit of string or a clasp. And the Jews of ancient Greece who wanted their sons to be top athletes would purposely avoid circumcising their lads in order to enable them to do this.

It used to be thought that a circumcised penis was healthier and cleaner than an uncircumcised one. But these days evidence proves that it is a totally unnecessary snip that gains you nothing and might even lose you a point or two.

The head of a penis which still has a foreskin is slightly more sensitive to touch and sensation than one which has had its protective skin removed. No big deal though. And equally, as long as you take baths and wash regularly under your foreskin, there is no reason to assume a circumcised willy will be more hygienic than an uncircumcised one. So, it's swings and roundabouts.

The stuff that does collect under the foreskin of an uncircumcised willy is pretty evil goo called smegma.

Also known as 'knob cheese', this whitish, waxy deposit can get very smelly, very quickly, locked away under the warm sweaty darkness of the foreskin. And it can cause some fairly nasty bacteria to grow. But that's at its very worst. As long as you keep it clean, a foreskin is a very useful thing to have.

On a fairly gruesome note, apart from anything else, should you ever need extra skin for some emergency skin-grafting operation, you've got a ready-made square inch or so to spare!

Traditionally, ritual religious circumcisions are carried out by an officer of that religion or in African tribes by a senior tribal figure. In years past, these vital snips might have been made with anything from sharpened bones to a rabbi's toughened thumbnail. But these days, the operations which are carried out on babies in hospital normally use the 'bell clamp' method, which doesn't involve an anaesthetic. A thing like a thimble is put over the head of the penis and the foreskin is pulled over the top. Then another part of the device is clamped down on the foreskin, cutting it off.

Medical reasons to give your willy a round neck and short sleeves

Older boys and men are normally only circumcised when there's a medical reason for it. Usually this is because the foreskin doesn't fit the penis properly. Phimosis is the name of the condition where the foreskin can't be properly pulled back over the helmet or glans of the penis. This is either because there's an excess of foreskin or else the foreskin is too tight.

Having a foreskin which is too tight is like trying to get a polo neck that's shrunk by two sizes over your head. It's a painful condition which can make masturbating or sex very sore. But the good news is that circumcision is a simple operation; you should be in and out of hospital on the same day. And after being circumcised, everything should be back, firing on all cylinders and fully operational, within about two weeks.

A slightly worse version of the 'two sizes too small polo neck syndrome' is paraphimosis. What happens here is that the foreskin is pulled back over the helmet of the penis and then gets stuck. What this does is cause the glans to swell up and stop the foreskin shifting back to its normal position. Again, a quick trip to the doctor and a bit of clever circumcision in surgery and you'll have a funny-looking bald-headed man for a willy, but no more nasty cramped sensations in the trouser department.

With all these knob problems, the same rule applies: the sooner they're treated the less trouble they are to deal with.

Circumcision correspondence

Most of the letters I get about circumcision are from boys who have experienced some pain and tightness of the foreskin and don't know what to do, but think they should have the offending skin removed. As always, I encourage them to seek the advice of their doctor.

Strangely enough, there is the occasional boy who thinks that to be circumcised is pretty cool and will help enhance his sex life:

> This may sound really stupid but I want to get circumcised. All my older brothers are, but for some reason I'm not. I think mine looks ugly and both my previous and present

girlfriends refuse to give me oral sex because of that. I was wondering if it was possible to get circumcised on the NHS.

Duncan (18)

But usually the letters are from boys who have been circumcised and who wish they hadn't, because they think of themselves as being abnormal:

● When I was younger I was circumcised, I don't know why because I'm not Jewish and I'm embarrassed to ask my parents why I was circumcised. When I was younger I thought I was deformed. It's really awful as my ex-girlfriend found out, and when we finished she told everyone. Now I can't go anywhere without people laughing and sniggering at me.

Depressed (14)

● I'm embarrassed. I've been circumcised. I had this done when I was seven and now I'm twelve. I've recently reached puberty which makes things worse. At my school it's some sort of custom after games lessons during showers to parade around naked to show off what they've got or haven't got. I'm afraid that if boys see what I've got they will laugh and tease me and most of all tell girls about me having been circumcised.

Pete

The fear of girls finding out about being circumcised is a very common one. So strong is this assumed image of abnormality that some boys seem to think circumcision will make them unacceptable and unlovable.

They think being circumcised will spoil their chances of having a normal sex life:

● My girlfriend keeps asking me to have sex with her, but as much as I want to, I refuse. I have a problem. I have been circumcised and if I tell her she is sure to dump me. I am desperate.

Anon

● I am sixteen and I had a sexual relationship with my girlfriend who is nineteen. I was shocked when I discovered that the foreskin on my penis was too tight and I had to have a circumcision. I am very embarrassed because my penis looks very peculiar. My girlfriend has been pressuring me into continuing our sexual relationship. What should I do? She does not know of my operation and I don't want to tell her as I think she would leave me.

Concerned

Nothing cuts deeper into the psyche of the male mind than the knob. So important is the penis to some males that everything else gets overlooked. You could be the cleverest, funniest, most charming and approachable boy in the world, but if you allow yourself to get hung up about something to do with your dick, it can completely blow your self confidence.

The idea that being circumcised or having a slightly smaller than average penis can totally affect girls' feelings towards you is madness. It really just isn't such a big deal and doesn't seem to be a factor of importance on any girl's agenda. But boys who are locked into that prick=power=personality way of thinking can't see the truth of it. And what makes it worse is they feel they can't talk about their pricks, their fears or their problems. They can't talk to mates, because they'll laugh, or to girls because they'll reject them, or to parents because they won't understand or think it's important, or to doctors because they're too embarrassed.

The truth is, willies are not such a big thing as you think they are. And the more frank you are about your frankfurter or direct about your dick, the easier it is for others to help or be understanding. The more of a meal you make about your member, the more you get hung up and embarrassed about it.

So if your dick is giving you stick, don't suffer in silence. Talk about it, moan about it, wave it at a doctor. Don't just hide it down your Y-fronts and hope it'll get better.

We've all got them, they're dead daft, but they can be a lot of fun too. Wear your plonker with pride.

The dick and the *doctor*

Given that such a large percentage of boys have a bit of a penis obsession, always worrying about the size of it, the shape of it and its ability to function, you'd think they'd never be out of the doctor's waiting room.

In fact, considering that so many obviously consider it to be the most important treasure they possess and the ultimate key to the sexual universe, you'd think they'd be getting it checked out by the professionals practically every other day. You'd think they'd treat it like a thoroughbred racehorse or Formula One racing car, employing a full-time vet or mechanic just to keep it in tip-top, highly tuned, A1 condition. You'd expect men to be knob hypochondriacs of the very first order.

The truth is that men and boys all too rarely go to the doctor for medical advice or treatment for their tackle. Even when they're suffering a lot of pain and heaps of worry.

So intense is the pride and embarrassment surrounding the penis that some males will suffer all manner of horrible pain and worry, before being forced to admit what's going on.

> For about three years now I have had four lumps in my penis. They are quite near the top and they are loose under the skin. I can feel them. I am a very nervous sixteen-year-old, so I could not possibly go to the doctor. The thing is me and my girlfriend are talking about sex. Is there a cream I could buy to clear this up?
>
> *Concerned*

The truth is that *any* lumps or bumps on the penis or testicles need to be shown to a doctor. It's impossible for any agony aunt or uncle to decipher or diagnose medical matters from letters. And they shouldn't be dealing with medical stuff anyway, it's strictly for the experts – in other words, doctors.

Maybe there's something the medical profession could do to make themselves more approachable. Or maybe we males need to get real about our priorities. What's worse – feeling a tad embarrassed about showing your todger to a quack, or spending sleepless nights and aching days worrying that your beloved bazooka is about to drop off?

Even basic problems like having a foreskin that's too tight, which could easily be solved by a simple circumcision, will be suffered in silence without consulting a doctor:

● I am fifteen. I have an embarrassing problem: I have a tight foreskin. I have known about it for two years and in this time I have not really been near a girl. At first I thought it would grow, but as time goes on I am less optimistic. What shall I do? It has shattered my confidence. I do not want to go to a doctor.

Worried of Wales

● I am thirteen and very worried about my penis. My foreskin is very tight and I'm not able to get the tip or helmet of my penis out. A friend said it should loosen in time. I'm too scared to see a doctor. Does being overweight have anything to do with it?

Anon

● I am fifteen. At school people brag about how far they can pull their foreskins back, saying they can get it right back to the hilt. I am worried because I can only pull it back a small way and daren't take it past the edge of my helmet for fear of not being able to get it back. Should I worry or are my schoolmates lying?

David

Just in the same way as some people can touch their nose with their tongue or bend their thumb back to touch their wrist, so some lads' tackle does different things from other lads'. It doesn't mean it's any less efficient or fun to own.

Having a foreskin which is noticeably tighter than other boys' or worrying that yours feels tighter is another example of how playground, back-of-the-

Portakabin banter doesn't help. If you've got a worry about your whanger and can talk to someone sensible about it – an uncle, father, teacher, doctor, or whoever – they can put your mind at rest or even get you medical help if you need it. Whereas a lot of your leery mates might just enjoy helping you believe that you're a space alien with a freaky flapper which is only fit to get you a guest slot on *That's Life*.

As with all penis and sex matters, having friends who brag and make up stories doesn't help, because it makes you nervous about telling the truth. There's no animal on the face of the earth who has the potential for being so cruel, thoughtless and unsympathetic as the teenage male, especially when found in groups.

So boys are often not only no help when it comes to solving each other's worries and problems, they can often make things much worse. It's par for the course to wind each other up and tease anyone who is genuinely concerned or has something unusual about his tackle. This understandably makes boys wary about being vulnerable.

Warts and all

Spots, warts and moles are all very common additions to the average willy. They occur for a variety of straightforward reasons. Many are easy to deal with and in fact some you can just ignore. But nobody tells us this. Nobody takes you to one side when you're eleven and says, 'Now, seeing as you're the owner of a fine willy, it's essential you know a few of the things that might go wrong in the years to come.'

I mean, even if you buy a bike, a car or a computer, you get given an *Owner's Manual* with a complete fault-finding guide and chapters of recommended remedies. Not so with the knob. Get born with one of those and it's pretty much up to you to learn how it works. Guidance is not very forthcoming.

In my opinion girls get a much better deal because: a) they can get pregnant, so parents take much more care and consideration about making sure they know the ins and outs of their bodies and about contraception; and b) they have periods. Periods are significant because they mark a specific day on which a girl's body starts to undergo changes. She is turning into a woman, therefore her mum, teachers, sister or whoever, knows that, if they haven't already done so, now is the right time to take her to one side and explain about what's happening to her body, and what's going to happen.

Boys don't have periods. That doesn't mean their bodies don't undergo some pretty radical changes. Some amazing things do happen during puberty, like the development of the genitals.

As a foetus, a boy's balls are up inside his body. During late pregnancy they drop into the scrotal sac. Usually, they will have descended by the time the baby is born. During puberty the sac will start to hang lower, the balls get slowly bigger and the skin around them gets baggier. In time one testicle starts to hang lower than the other – usually the left one. One testicle might grow faster than another and seem bigger, but eventually in adulthood they'll normally equal out to the same size.

During puberty the whole trouser department goes through a complete refurbishing. Your balls get lower and bigger, your scrotum skin gets darker in colour, your penis gets thicker and more pronounced. And, of course, the whole shooting match gets hairier. It happens to different boys at different times and at different rates. There's no such thing as normal.

Everyone's individual, so rather than worry that your tackle's not the same as the next guy's, just chill out and wait to see what develops.

But because boys' body changes *are* gradual and happen slowly, no adult or parent has to decide when it is a good time to sit a lad down and tell him about what to expect and what might be going to happen to his tackle.

Is it any wonder then that we get worried?

One of the most common medical worries is spots on the tackle:

● I'm a normal fifteen-year-old boy who has a worrying problem. On my testicles and underside of my penis I have got hundreds of little pimples. They are only tiny but quite numerous. They are normal skin-coloured and don't seem disgusting or obscene. They're not scabby. Are they harmful or just natural?

Ben

● I am fourteen and very confused. When I masturbate, which I do very often, little white pimples show up on my foreskin and penis. I'm scared that my girlfriend will see them and no longer want me. I don't want to see my doctor as he's a close family friend.

Ian

● I am fourteen with a very worrying problem. On my penis I have little goose-pimple-like spots that are yellowy in colour. I've had these spots for about a year. I'm too embarrassed to tell my mother or go to a doctor. It's really starting to worry me.

Joe

Little spots and bumps that appear on the penis and balls are normally either hair follicles or sweat glands beginning to develop. They can look like a weird kind of whitish or creamy rash. Some are bigger than others, but usually there's hundreds of them.

It's easy to think that there may be something desperately wrong or else you've caught some horrid disease. In fact it's just pubic hairs trying to push up through the skin, or else oil and perspiration glands coming to life to do their bit.

Your perspiration glands develop as you grow through puberty and so do the oil glands. It's the production of all this oil and sweat stuff that also gives you pimples on your face. The over-production causes the pores to get blocked. It's a bit of a drag when it's developing but we need the oil to keep our skin supple and need the sweat glands to keep us cool. It would be an even bigger drag if your face crumbled away from being dry and every time you walked into a crowded room you fainted from the heat!

Warts

Warts on the willy are very common. They can get together and form a cluster or else there can be solitary, lone warts which take root and stand proud, causing their owner no end of consternation. Warts can come and go. Or they can dig in for the duration, never changing or shifting. They can appear on the foreskin, the helmet, balls, shaft or even inside the penis, down the urethra. They can be small, flat and smooth or large pink cauliflower lumps. They can even sometimes be too small to see at all. They can sting like hell or else give absolutely no sensation at all.

But whatever they do, you can bet your granny's life savings they will make the wart wearer *worry*.

● I am seventeen and still a virgin. I'm frightened to go out with girls because I have three black warts on my penis which are very large and very noticeable.

Anon

● I've got a very embarrassing problem. I've got a very big wart near the end of my penis. It doesn't hurt but I'm scared to tell anyone. I told my best mate and he's told his father who's a doctor. Now I feel as if I'll die if he mentions it.

Martin

Although genital warts can be sexually transmitted, you don't have to have had sex to get them. They can grow all by themselves. They are really very easy to treat if they're shown to a doctor. Usually, external warts can be coated with a paint-on lotion which the doctor'll prescribe and after a few treatments they just fall off. Otherwise they can sometimes be frozen off, burned off or even zapped with laser treatment. It all sounds much more exotic and painful than it really is. The removal of warts is not a big deal and is very, very common.

But if you don't get them dealt with they can multiply and spread. And if you do have genital warts and you have sex, not only can you pass them on, they might also do greater harm to the poor girl who you give them to. Certain types of genital warts have been linked to cervical cancer in women.

Keeping your tackle clean and healthy and getting it checked out by a doctor is not just important for the owner's peace of mind, it's also important for your partner if you do start having sex. Being a bit scared and embarrassed about going to the doctor is not only bad for your health – it could also be bad for the health of someone you love.

Things that won't go away

If you manage to persuade yourself that there's no way you can take your todger to the doctor, then you could be setting up your equipment and your sex life for serious trouble. In certain severe cases you risk losing your tackle completely and with a lot of infections you could end up infertile and even impotent.

Sexually transmitted diseases (STDs) fall into two main categories: bacterial and viral. The bacterial ones live on the surface of the skin. They are quite easy to treat and can be cured completely. But viral ones get into the cells of the body and are very hard to get rid of. They can keep coming back. Ignoring these diseases will only let them get worse and worse. The best way to deal with any sort of infection is to catch it quick before it has time to do any lasting damage. But that means you have to seek treatment from a doctor.

Hoping and praying is not good treatment. Making an appointment is.

Unusual itching, redness, pain from peeing, coloured discharge and a nasty smell under the foreskin are all symptoms of sexually transmitted diseases. They're also things that a lot of boys have had and have chosen to ignore. Symptoms are a clue as to what's going on. If they're ignored, it doesn't mean the cause is going to clear up and the cause could be serious. There's a whole hamper of diseases you can get through your dick:

Syphilis (the pox)   A pretty rare disease these days. But it's a bad one if you try and ignore it. The results of long-term infection can lead to blindness and senility. The symptoms are a painless, clearly visible, ulcer which appears on the penis two to four weeks after sex. But a course of antibiotics can sort it out, if dealt with early on.

Gonorrhoea (the clap)   Another old-fashioned disease that looked to be beaten until recently, when it started to make a strong comeback. A yellowy white discharge from the penis that doesn't smell is the most common symptom. This is matched with some pain when peeing and even some flu-like feelings. Some men don't show any symptoms at all. Not only can it eventually cause inflammation and abscesses of the testicles with the threat of losing a testicle, but if it is transmitted to pregnant women it can infect their babies. Antibiotics are enough to sort it out.

Genital herpes   Get herpes and you've got it for life. They are small sore blisters that appear on the penis. They fill with a clear liquid that turns yellow and when they burst the remaining ulcers dry and develop a scab. All this is usually accompanied by flu-like symptoms and irritation around the tackle. There is no known cure but anti-viral drugs can minimize the nastiness and frequency of the attacks. Obviously it's better not to get it at all. It is usually caught from somebody with a sore on their genitals or from oral sex with somebody with a cold sore.

Pubic lice You don't just get these little crab-like creatures from having sex with someone who already has them. You can catch them off bedding, clothes and towels too. The little beggers live in your pubic hair and suck your blood. The way you know you've got them is that you itch like anything and then you notice them crawling about. A trip to the doctor will get you a lotion to apply which will kill them off. If you *don't* deal with them they'll spread to your eyebrows, underarms and eyelashes, causing you to itch for England.

Scabies You don't have to have sex to acquire this scrotum scratching sensation. Scabies is another major itching problem caused by a little mite burrowing into the skin to lay eggs. You need to get a lotion from the doctor or else this parasite will spread all over your body.

Thrush This bacteria occurs naturally in a woman's vagina and usually does no harm. Sometimes it can multiply and cause infection which a man can catch under his foreskin. Men can get thrush, or a sort of similar bacterial infection, without having sex as well. A redness and itchiness under the foreskin is the normal sign. Cream can clear it up. If it's not treated you can just go on reinfecting your partner, who'll just go on giving it back to you.

Urethritis (NSU – Non-specific Urethritis) If it feels like you're peeing razor blades, then you might have NSU. It's an infection of the urethra, which is the tube that runs the length of the penis carrying urine from the bladder. Any pus visible at the end of the penis is a clue, as is aching balls or pain during sex. It's treated easily with antibiotics, but if it's ignored it can affect the testicles so badly that one might have to be removed. And if passed on to women it can cause infertility.

Jock Itch This delightfully named nasty is also known as Jock Rot, because it's often caught by lads who do a lot of sporty, athletic things. It's nothing to do with sex. It's a fungal infection caused by getting damp and sweaty a lot and not drying the skin properly. It can also be caused by wearing too tight trousers or underpants which don't allow the air to circulate properly. It comes up as an itchy redness around the genitals. Dusting with talcum powder might be enough to stop it. Otherwise anti-fungal powders and creams can be got from the chemist.

HIV (Human Immunodeficiency Virus) HIV is the virus which can lead to AIDS. It's a virus which attacks the white cells in the blood, eventually killing so many that the body can't protect itself from infections. A number of people who get HIV go on to develop AIDS. This often means they contract serious illnesses like pneumonia, and because their body has lost its natural defence mechanism, the diseases can prove fatal.

Two ways you can get HIV are from having unprotected sex and sharing syringe needles with an infected person. The needles can transfer the virus because they have traces of infected blood on them. Sex can transfer HIV because spunk (or semen as it's properly known), menstrual blood and vaginal juices can all carry the virus.

Oral, anal or vaginal sex with an infected person can transfer HIV. Using a condom lessens the risk. You can't get HIV from shaking hands, sharing towels, sitting on loo seats, eating off crockery or any other everyday things. But you can get it from sex. And the thing is, you can't tell if someone has the virus. It has no outward visible symptoms. The only way people find out if they've been infected is to get a test. And obviously, if it shows up positive, it's too late. HIV is invisible but deadly. It's not worth taking chances with.

Just think of your dick as a Jaguar XJ6 4.2 litre, fuel injected, Sovereign saloon car, which the Jaguar manufacturers gave you for free. They also said that you could get it mended or serviced, without charge, whenever you want. Just ring the Jag Freephone number and they'll do it the same day – right?

So, you've got this totally brilliant motor. The dog's bollocks. The business. Great. It'll do 130 mph top whack, cruise at 95 mph and glide round corners like ice cream on a hot plate. Look after it and this car will give you years of intense pleasure. You can share it with people you really like, give them pleasure too. Every time you use it you can feel a warm glow of satisfaction.

It's got to be worth looking after – hasn't it?

Now imagine if it were to go wrong. One day it starts smoking out the exhaust and juddering when you put your foot down. Maybe one of your passengers points out it's not sounding as smooth as it normally does. What do you do? Ignore it and hope it gets better? Give up driving this beautiful motor for ever? Or phone the Freephone?

Of course you'd phone. They said they'd mend it. You know you'll soon be back on the motorway having a wonderful time after they've tinkered. So you'd phone, no question. Blimey, if the thing even so much as coughed you'd be round that Jag garage faster than a whippet with the runs, to get it looked at.

But sadly, when it comes to looking after their penises, this fabulous organ that could supply decades of indescribably exciting pleasure, so many men just never pick up that phone or visit the garage.

Look after your willy and it'll look after you.

The Willy in Action

4

*Erect*ions

I can clearly remember, aged about four, sitting on my bedroom floor in my pyjamas, prodding me todger with a Lego block. A few prods and the little pink thing would feel funny and start to go stiff. It was a whole lot of fun and much more interesting than building Lego models. Which, apart from anything else, is probably the main reason I didn't become a famous architect. If only I'd been less interested in my willy.

Early erections are strange because although you know they feel nice, you don't really know why they do or what's going on. There was this pole in my mum's garden which she used to tie up the washing line. As a five-year-old I would shunt up it, clamping it in my hands, between my feet and through my groin. The sensation of climbing this pole felt very nice, much nicer than any other climbing experience I ever had. I'd no idea why. The fact that it rubbed against my willy as I shunted meant nothing. I didn't really connect the sensations.

Even running very fast as a pre-adolescent could make me experience that same warm excited feeling at the bottom of my tummy. Presumably the sensation of my thighs rubbing together excited my penis. But I didn't know. Didn't have a clue.

That's the thing about erections, for the first few years you live in blissful ignorance of what they are and why they happen, you just get to enjoy the occasional yummy sensations. Then you find out what they are. You learn about their sexual significance and taboo reputation, and suddenly you're thrown into a mass of embarrassment and shame every time you get one:

● I am sixteen and need help desperately. I just can't stop getting erections. I embarrassed my girlfriend in front of her parents. I just can't control it. I daren't go swimming because people will see me and laugh. My life is a complete misery. Do all boys go through this? Am I abnormal? I feel so dirty.

Nick

● I have this terrible problem that I can't talk to anyone about as it is embarrassing. Every time I see this girl I have an erection. I can't control it. A lot of people might think I'm disgusting but I can't help myself. Please help, I'm becoming suicidal.

Jim

● I am a boy of fourteen and three-quarters. I don't know what to do. My penis keeps becoming erect whenever it feels like it. It's got a mind of its own. I think of something boring or a lesson but nothing happens, it doesn't go down. I'm scared someone will notice and I'll get embarrassed, so I have to cover my waist with something.

Leeds fan

The reason why an erection is embarrassing is because it's seen as an indication of sexual goings on. Supposedly, the idea is that if you've got a hard-on then you must be having sexy and therefore naughty thoughts. So the embarrassment is about other people knowing what you're thinking, particularly as it's of such an intimate nature.

The ironic truth is that you could be thinking about carpet tiles and still get a stiffy. If your willy has got an urge to stand up, then it really doesn't matter what's going on in your mind, it's going to do what it wants to do.

It's the shame connected with erections which is such a hard thing to accept. Every normal male experiences a lot more erections than are required for having sex. We all have had stiffies at times when they're definitely not required. But even though they're an everyday occurrence there's still a whole lot of fuss made about them. They are very common, very natural things to have, but they often get regarded as terrible, rude and offensive.

It is absolutely illegal to show an erect penis on television or in a mainstream publication. Why? You're allowed to show naked breasts, exposed pubic mounds, even limp willies. But as soon as they become erect, suddenly they become illegal. What's the big deal? Why does their texture make such a difference? Obviously it's because of what an erect penis represents, i.e. a male sex organ ready for sex.

Is it any wonder boys get embarrassed about having unwanted erections when so much fuss is being made about a straight-up todger? And, of course, it doesn't help when other people point it out:

● I'm fifteen and just about every time I get on a bus I get an erection. I went on a bus with my girlfriend into town and when she noticed she wouldn't stop laughing at me. Everybody turned round and there was I with this lump pointing up at me from my trousers. I wanted to die. Is there something wrong with me?

Embarrassed

● I am a fourteen-year-old boy and my girlfriend was telling me a story of two people making love. As she told me I got an erection. When she noticed my erection she was cross and now thinks I'm sex mad. And she's told everyone at school and now I'm a laughing stock.

Jason

Buses and coaches can be a nightmare in the unwanted erections department. There's something about the throb and vibrations of diesel engines that can easily entice an erection. You might be totally unaware of anything, just happily minding your own business on your way to school, and suddenly realize you've got a stiffy.

Erections can creep up on you when you least expect them:

● I am an eighteen-year-old and I'd like to know if it's normal to have erections an average of eight or nine times a day without physical stimulation? Do I have too many erections? Even when I am not thinking of sex, like when I'm sitting playing the piano during music lessons, I get erections. Is this harmful?

John

Unwanted erections can be annoying, they can be embarrassing if noticed and they can be uncomfortable. But let's not get carried away with their importance; they can also be dealt with fairly easily. Erections become most noticeable and most inconvenient when they have room to manoeuvre.

If you've got really baggy boxer shorts or loose tracksuit bottoms, then there's nothing to stop the stiffy sticking out. Some boys find it helps to wear more constricting briefs, or even two pairs of briefs, when they're going through a particularly active phase in the trouser department. Wearing a jock strap can also be an effective way of restraining a wild willy.

Hiding unwanted erections is not really that difficult, so long as you've got your clothes on. But there are times when you haven't got anything to hide what's going on. A lot of boys experience problems with over-proud penises when they are naked in the communal showers at school:

Please don't laugh at me. My problem started a few months ago during the rugby season at school. I was in the showers after a match when I got an erection. Everyone started to laugh at me and called in other people to see. I ran out of the showers on the verge of tears, got dressed and ran home. When I went back to school everyone laughed at me and called me names. I am dreading the next time I have to go into the showers with other people. I don't understand how it happened, I'm sure I'm not gay. I feel so depressed I want to die.

Anon

Instead of just being an embarrassing lump in your trousers, an erection can be an excruciatingly embarrassing reality in an all-male environment. Mainly because boys are so frightened of being thought of as gay by their peers. They're frightened because of all the stick and mickey-taking they'd have to put up with.

When you think about it, getting an erection in the showers is not that surprising. If geography lessons and coach trips can get you hard, even without thinking, it's not that unlikely warm showers will work too.

Also, whether you like it or not, being naked in amongst other naked bodies, even if they are your own sex and you consider yourself to be heterosexual, can be a stimulating experience. Especially during your adolescent years, when your hormones are working overtime anyway, the sensation of stripping off and then getting into the shower can have an arousing effect on your penis. Even if you're completely repelled by the whole idea of naked men's bodies and communal bathing, your knob doesn't necessarily know that. We've all experienced a thousand erections at totally inappropriate times and situations; this is just another example.

Getting a stiffy in the showers at school doesn't mean you're gay or attracted to men's bodies. All it means is that your tackle is working well, it's doing all the things it's supposed to, it's just doing a spot of overtime. Not a problem. Not abnormal. Just a healthy, happy horn, doing its thing.

Morning *glories*

There are times when you don't want an erection, whether it's in the changing rooms or the school bus. There are times when you do want a stiffy and you can't get one, often during your first sexual experiences. And there is one time when nearly every male gets an erection regardless: first thing in the morning.

Waking up with a stonker is very common. These early morning erections are sometimes called 'piss-hards', because people assume that they've got something to do with the build-up of pressure in your bladder overnight. But there isn't any evidence to prove this is the case. What is much more likely is that it's simply the leftovers from the last dream you had.

When you dream, you'll often get an erection. This might happen up to five or six times a night and no one really knows why. It doesn't mean you're dreaming about sex. On the contrary, you might be having nightmares, or not remember the dreams at all, yet still your knob'll stand to attention. Waking up with a stiffy might make you want to masturbate, but strangely enough, often the first erection of the day isn't a very sensual one. And usually if you ignore it, it'll soon go limp and let you get on with life.

Wet dreams

The scary thing about wet dreams is not so much that they happen, but the fact that no one bothers to warn you that they might happen.

The first time I woke up with a puddle of spunk on my pyjamas I was frankly amazed. I could see it wasn't wee, I *knew* it was semen, but I couldn't think how or why it was there. I had no recollection of any dream, I just woke up sticky.

Many boys between the ages of twelve and fifteen will experience wet dreams. Some might have loads of them and some might not have any. Personally, I can only lay claim to ever having two. One I can remember was accompanied by a sexy dream, the other – nothing.

Physically speaking, all that's going on is that your sperm-producing equipment is having a bit of a test run. It's doing a quick once round the track while you're asleep, to check out the motor and make sure the spunk manufacture and distribution network is all properly in place.

It's a perfectly natural, subconscious way for the body to empty your semen stores, in order to start up production again. Sometimes you get an added bonus and a sexy dream to go with the clear-out and some-times you don't.

Often boys will experience their first-ever ejacu-lation through a wet dream. The first time they ever come could be through this mechanism of subcon-scious triggering. Boys who masturbate regularly tend to have fewer wet dreams, although you can have both.

So the first time you ever come might be a complete surprise that happens in the middle of the night and leaves you waking up with a puddle of stuff you've never seen before sticking to your sheets. To think that nobody takes the trouble to warn you about this is a bit out of order really. It could frighten the life out of you!

Lots of boys it's happened to think they've wet themselves or else think they've been bleeding through their dick. Some even think they've done something really terrible and that this is the punishment.

Whether or not you know what the physical reason for your coming in the night was, the sense of embarrassment is always very strong and the practicalities of what to do about the sheets are also a big issue:

● I've been going through a phase of wet dreams which I can't control. One morning my sister caught me trying to hide the sheets and threatened to tell our mum and dad. I don't want her to tell Mum and Dad what I'm going through.

Confused

● I am fourteen. A few nights ago I woke up to find that my bed was damp. My mum asked me why it was wet, so I told her I had wee'd in it overnight. She was very cross and told me I shouldn't be doing this at my age. The truth is I don't think I did wee in my bed. Could this have been a wet dream? If so, what exactly is one and why do we have them? My friends always laugh and joke about them at school but I don't really know what they are.

Embarrassed

Any damp patches that you find in bed in the morning which have got nothing to do with wee, are very likely to be semen. Nocturnal ejaculations of semen can't be controlled, they're not your 'fault', they're not dirty or bad or anything to be scared of. They can be a tad messy, but wearing underpants in bed if they happen a bit frequently will soon solve that problem.

Some boys worry when they either have wet

dreams at a young age or continue to have them as they get older. But you can go on having wet dreams occasionally all of your life, although your teens are usually the busiest time:

● I have started having wet dreams but I haven't really started puberty yet. Nobody else in my form has had a wet dream apart from me. Why is this?

Chris (13)

● I have wet dreams occasionally but I've heard that these aren't real sperm. I'm concerned because I thought these only lasted through puberty and now I'm seventeen.

Luke

There are some boys who worry about having too many wet dreams:

● My problem is I keep having wet dreams. I can't help it. I usually have one every night. Is there any way I can stop them? One of my friends said that if you were having them you would run out of sperm and therefore not get a girl pregnant. When I'm married I do want a baby, will all these wet dreams cause a problem for this?

Lee (15)

On the other hand, some boys are mortified that they're missing out by not having any:

● I know this might sound stupid but I am a seventeen-year-old lad and I have never had a wet dream. What is the cause of this?

All my friends have had wet dreams but I haven't. Could this be because I am overweight?

Anon

Like everything else to do with the willy, wet dreams get confusing. Some boys go on bragging about how many wet dreams they've had and how brilliant they were. While other boys feel racked with guilt and shame and try and cover up the fact that it's happened.

In some ways wet dreams are the nearest equivalent to a girl's periods. If a boy has a wet dream, it might be the first ever ejaculation he has, and so it marks the start of puberty. Girls get periods explained to them by mothers, aunts, sisters, teachers, magazines and even TV adverts. What do most boys get? A sticky willy and a lot of worry.

It's the same old story. When it comes to growing up with a willy, most of the time you just have to guess and make it up as you go along. Because no one tells you anything.

Mas*tur*bation

I got taught how to wank. I had a mate called Mervyn who was very advanced in the sex self-exploration field. And anyway Merv told me about this great new sport I was missing. When I voiced an interest, he obligingly showed me how to do it. Good old Merv, he set me up for life. I can't say I've looked back since. I certainly haven't stopped.

Although, I have to admit, it wasn't all plain sailing

from the word go. Even though I could get a hard on easily by a bit of fiddling and diddling and even though I definitely enjoyed banging the old bishop, I got no end result. When Merv reached the climax of his doings, he'd spurt a glob of come, but not me. The well was dry. At the tender age of eleven, my testicles weren't producing any semen to create an ejaculation. This worried me. It didn't put me off beating me meat, but I wasn't quite sure why I couldn't come up with the creamy white goods like Merv.

It didn't take very long before I'd forgotten I was worried, because soon enough I was churning out the old love juice and was as happy as a sandboy eagerly playing with my new toy.

Before I was shown what to do, I knew a bit about getting a stiffy, I knew what sex was, but I had no idea about wanking. Although it's a bit embarrassing to think about how I found out, thankfully I haven't seen Merv for about twenty years so it's not a big deal. But in many ways I have a lot to thank him for, because since then no one has *ever* talked to me about masturbation.

I had some really awful sex education at school, but the biology teacher never mentioned the old handy shandy once. A teacher talking about sex education but not including masturbation! Pretty poor.

And not surprisingly it's yet another one of those secret male things that no one really talks about properly. Sure we all call each other 'wankers' as an insult and might joke about the practice of pulling the plonker. But there's no reassurance or honest talk about what it is lads do under the privacy of their own duvet.

Luckily, I grew up thinking of it as a very normal and pleasant pastime and managed to devote a huge part of my teenage time and energy to eagerly pummelling my mutton.

I was lucky. A lot of boys get very screwed up about masturbation:

● I am fourteen and I masturbate every day, sometimes twice or even three times. I have noticed my penis sometimes feels sore. Am I doing it any harm? Does this mean I'll use up my sperms and not be able to father children?

Very worried

● I am twenty and still a virgin. I think I masturbate too much. As soon as I wake up I masturbate and then after each meal. I also masturbate when I go to bed at night. Do you think I'm abnormal?

Ben

One of the most common worries is not so much about the *act* of masturbation but how often it's 'allowed' or 'healthy' to do it. The truth is there's no medical reason why masturbating four times a day will do you any harm. And probably most boys go through a phase of flogging the dolphin like it's going out of fashion. But usually it's just a phase and things calm down again later, then they might pick up for a spurt at another juncture. Frequency is not a real problem unless wanking becomes obsessive.

Compulsive masturbation, when you just do it continually for the escapism of giving continuous self-pleasure is spooky, but up to five times a day is just youthful dedication.

So some guys get to feel guilty about fiddling with the fun rod, because they're scared about what it's doing to their bodies. Others get scared because of what it's doing to their souls:

In my religion masturbation is seen as a sin. I have masturbated lots of times but I really try hard not to. I hate myself for doing it but I can't find it in me to resist. I must be weak and bad. I don't know who to tell.

Anon (15)

And some boys are made to feel bad about stirring their stew by others:

I am fifteen and my mum caught me masturbating. She thinks it's dirty and I should be ashamed of myself. I don't think I should because my friends still do it and I've read that it's good for you. My mum said she'll kick me out. What should I do?

Steve

Being caught having a wank seems to be something that a lot of boys fear, and some have unfortunately experienced:

About two weeks ago I was getting ready to go out on a date with my girlfriend. I went into the shower and got undressed not knowing I hadn't locked the bathroom door. I washed and turned the shower off, then had an urge to masturbate. My neighbour was downstairs chatting to my mum; when she came upstairs to use the toilet she came in and caught me masturbating.

Embarrassed

I am sixteen and my thirteen-year-old sister caught me masturbating in the bathroom. It was very embarrassing and now

everyone at the Sixth Form I attend knows
about it. I'm really depressed.

Man United supporter

Knowing we all wank is one thing, but being caught
in the act is another. It's still not a very serious business
really. The moral of the tale is that you should take
care where you have a wank. It's something that we
do in private for our own pleasure, so if you're running the risk of being caught by leaving the door
unlocked then maybe you're after extra thrills. Maybe
you *want* to be caught. In which case you're being
unfair, because then you're being an exhibitionist.
You're aiming to get thrills at the expense of shocking
someone else, which is well out of order.

You won't grow out of it

There's a bit of a myth which goes around that suggests tickling your pickle is only something you do
when you're a teenager. The implication is that when
you grow older and start having a regular 'real' sex
life, then you won't need to masturbate and so you'll
stop it for ever. This is total, undiluted tosh. Once a
wanker – always a wanker.

You might not varnish your pole quite as often
when you're in a sexual relationship as you did when
you were young, free and seriously single. But there's
absolutely no reason to suppose that you'll give it up.
Even if you're having top-class, rampant, athletic sex
every day of the week, it doesn't mean you won't
fancy a quick J. Arthur Rank once in a while.

It's a different kettle of fish. It's something you do
to relax or escape or enjoy a fantasy. So in that respect
it's completely different from the sex you might have
in a loving and caring relationship.

Some girls find it hard to understand how attached boys get to wonking their conker; they might even get upset and hurt by it:

◆ My boyfriend and I are both eighteen and have had a very active sex life. We normally make love about five or six times a week. So, it comes as a bit of a shock to me to find out that he still masturbates occasionally (normally on the first few days of my period when we don't make love). He says that if he doesn't relieve himself he gets a build-up of tension. Does this mean I'm not satisfying him? Or does he have abnormal needs?

Confused girlfriend

Sex and masturbation are definitely two different things. Maybe it's because we discover masturbation in our teens and have so much fun with it that it's hard to give up. And indeed, why should we? Most men will naturally go on shaking hands with Rosy Palm and her five little sisters until they basically can't get it up any more.

Wanking is good for you

Apart from being a cracking good way to pass a few minutes now and again, it can be argued that playing pocket billiards can actually be quite beneficial. During adolescence, when your hormones are working overtime and your sexual urges are going bananas, a wank can be a great comfort.

Masturbating is a good way of relieving sexual tension and frustration. Getting a grip on your dick can help you keep things in perspective and not get too worked up with sexual dissatisfaction. It's also a good way of getting to know your own sex organs. Wanking allows you to investigate your sexuality, both physically and mentally.

The way that you masturbate and bring yourself to the point of orgasm puts you in touch with what you like and how to achieve the most exciting orgasm. This sort of information can be a lot of use during sex. If you can guide a lover to touch and caress you in the way you find exciting, then it'll be exciting for them too. If you know your ins and outs, your nooks and crannies and your likes and dislikes, it all goes to help when making love.

As for your mental sexuality, the sort of things you think about while you're pulling your pudding are the things that turn you on, the fantasies that you like to explore.

Some boys can't be bothered to fantasize and they want pictures or videos to get them excited. Dirty mags have been the wanking fodder of men and boys since time began. But using dirty mags or dirty films is a bit of a lazy way to get yourself excited. Using your own mind and your own imagination to think up sexy scenes seems like a much more creative way of having a hand-gallop.

When fantasies aren't funny

Most of the time, wank fantasies are the things you enjoy while giving yourself manual pleasure. Usually they're secret little dreams involving people you know, people you've just met or else they might be film stars or celebrities, models or singers. And these sorts of mental images can be exciting and satisfying.

Some boys get worried though when their fantasies

don't fit the way they want to feel. The two sexual fantasies that seem to give boys the most trouble and concern are imagined sexy scenes with either sisters or best friends. These are very common fantasies. But what happens is that the person having one gets frightened because they imagine that these sexual fantasies are bad ones. Fantasizing about sex with your sister or sex with your best friend makes boys think they must be incest-crazed monsters or else potentially gay.

But a fantasy is just a fantasy. It's not reality. As long as you don't act on the fantasy, no one has been harmed and all that's happened is you've had some thoughts which have disturbed you. During your teens, as your sexuality is forming, it's very easy to get confused sexually. A huge number of boys and girls have feelings and fantasies about members of their own sex. They are just fantasies. Having these thoughts doesn't necessarily mean you are gay or going to be gay. At this stage of your life feelings of friendship and attraction can often get blurred and confused.

If you're having trouble with the fantasies that come into your head, then you can try using pictures for a while or try changing who and what you think about. Or even give up masturbating for a bit. The whole purpose of masturbation is to give yourself pleasure and comfort. If, for whatever reason, it isn't making you happy, then stop. It's not obligatory. You don't have to do it. Some people might be happier not wanking.

Wanking with friends

Male There are times when jerking the gherkin is not a solo pursuit. During adolescence, a lot of boys experiment with tossing off a friend or being tossed off by one. Often at boarding schools or on summer camps boys might get involved in wanking competitions or group masturbation activity. It's all very normal if a little bit embarrassing.

A lot of guys worry that because they've been experimenting sexually with other boys this means they'll grow up to be gay or they just worry that they've done something terrible. This sort of stuff goes on all the time. Most of what adolescent sex is about is experimentation and investigation. Boys and girls in single sex schools don't get the opportunity to experiment with the opposite sex as much as they'd like, so they do the next best thing.

Female The other type of shared masturbation is where you get tossed off by a girlfriend. Having a girl do what you've done a million times yourself gives the whole experience a brand-new and immensely exciting twist. A lot of boys love to have girls tickle their pickle.

But a lot of girls get into a panic because they worry that they won't know how to do it properly or will do something disastrously wrong:

> I'm a fifteen-year-old girl who has a lovely boyfriend. He keeps asking me to 'give him a wank' or 'toss him off' and I don't know what this means. I would be happy to do it if I knew what it was but I don't. I can't ask friends or family, it would be too embarrassing.
>
> *Cathy*

> I would like to know how to wank a boy off. I know it probably sounds silly, but a few nights ago my boyfriend asked me to,

and as I'd always read in magazines that it
was a very tender area I was extremely gentle.
I guess I was too gentle as he put his hand
on mine and applied more pressure. He applied
more and more pressure until he eventually
came. Now I don't know how much pressure
should be applied and how tender is the area.

Lucy (16)

I was at a party getting off with the boy
of my dreams when he asked me to 'toss
him off'. I was eager but scared I'd do
something stupid and I didn't and still don't
really know how. I quickly changed the subject
and we carried on, but all night he kept
pushing my hand nearer his penis. I want to
say yes, but I don't know what to do.

James Dean fan (15)

It is completely wrong and offensive for any boy to
expect or pressurize a girl into masturbating him. But
if both parties are willing then it makes a lot of sense
for a little communication to take place. How is a girl
supposed to know what you like? Girls are often more
scared of doing something wrong. The whole business
about this sort of sexual activity is that it should be
done in the most relaxed and exciting way. It's not
exciting if you're dead scared of making a fool of
yourself. But it is exciting to show carefully and share
what it is you want and even explain what it feels like
to be touched that way.

**The key to good sex is always good
communication. The more you can share your
experiences and communicate your desires
the better it will be. Wanking is something**

**you and your girlfriend can enjoy together, not
by just doing it but by talking about it too.**

*Ejac*ulation

We can send spacemen to the moon, dig tunnels
under the Channel, even design computers that'll
build Ford Sierras. But still we can't really compete
with the wonders of Mother Nature. In one single
ejaculation, in one simple wank's worth of come,
there are up to four million sperm. And it only takes
one sperm to fertilize a female's egg. Neat, eh?

Males tend to forget the wonders of spunk, probably because we see so much of it. It's easily possible
to come twice a day, 365 days of the year. That means
that in sixty years of sex and masturbation you could
come nearly 450,000 times. Which, if you average
about three and a half million sperm per come, means
that in a lifetime you could have ejaculated 13,500
billion sperm. This is some serious load.

The average portion of spunk is probably around a
teaspoonful in size. Sometimes it's more, sometimes
it's less. The amount usually only relates to how long
it's been since you last ejaculated. Also, as you get
older you might find that you don't produce so much,
so quickly. The peak of your come production is likely
to be in your teens and early twenties.

Sometimes your spunk will spurt out of your knob
like a greyhound launching itself out of the racing
traps. It might squirt a few feet, even whack you in
the face if you're having a wank. Other times it might
just dribble out the end in one small spurt, going
nowhere fast.

It can be thick and gloopy, almost yellow in colour,

while other times it's really thin and watery. In all these forms and quantities it's perfectly normal. And because sperm are microscopic, just a tiny bubble could still be brimming with millions of the little soldiers.

Spunk's got a salty taste and a strong sweetish smell.

Most of the worries that boys have concerning their ejaculations are either about not having started ejaculating at all, which is usually just the consequence of not starting puberty, or else they worry that they come too quickly during sex. And some even worry that they *can't* come during sex.

But even before sex rears its head, ejaculations can be a problem for other reasons.

⬤ I am a sixteen-year-old boy and the thing is I get erections very easily. Even just looking at a girl's chest makes a bulge in my trousers. That's not the problem, the problem is that when I get an erection I release a lot of sperm. It all seeps through my trousers and mates have even pointed it out and laughed. It sometimes looks like I've wet myself. The worst part is that when it dries it starts to smell.

Desperate

Although ejaculation is usually the end product of masturbation or sex, it can also happen just when the penis is aroused and erect. Often some semen will leak out of the end of your penis when you're getting excited. There's nothing you can do to stop it, it's like a pre-come come.

The important thing to realize though is that this pre-come semen can still contain millions of sperm, so it's just as likely to make a girl pregnant if accidentally transferred to the vagina on fingers.

A leaky dick can be an embarrassment, if it's going to spill some of its seeds early on in the proceedings or else leak during your afternoon woodwork lesson. But again, it's no big deal and will probably stop being so active as time wears on. If you do find you tend to cream the inside of your boxers regularly, then obviously it's important to change your underwear at least once a day, use deodorant and even maybe excuse yourself to go to the loo and mop up any excess with toilet paper. Chances are it won't happen that often or for a long period.

Ejaculation usually occurs when you reach a physical sexual climax either through wanking or sex or oral sex. And it's a very physical event: your heart rate and blood pressure increase, your breathing is often much faster than normal, and as you ejaculate, the muscles in your genital area contract and spunk is pumped out through your penis. It's a big occasion for the body and, because of what goes on, you usually get extremely pleasant sensations which create an intense moment called an orgasm.

Ejaculation is what happens to you physically; it's the act of spurting spunk. But an orgasm is what you *feel*. The two don't always go together. It is possible to have an orgasm and feel all those intense sensations and huge pleasures without ejaculating. And you can ejaculate without having the great feelings. Sometimes when you masturbate it's just a quick squirt with very little feeling at all. Yet sometimes great sex, maybe even sex without penetration, can be so sensual and exciting that you experience orgasmic feelings without ejaculating.

Alcohol doesn't normally help ejaculation or orgasm. Getting drunk can have disastrous short-term effects on your sex life. Too much drink can stop you coming, or can make you come very quickly. It can also affect your erection. 'Brewer's droop', where your dick becomes uncontrollably limp, is a common affliction. The fuzziness of alcohol can spoil an orgasm or inhibit it, or even just make you forget how nice it was. On the whole, booze and sex don't mix well.

A lot of people claim that getting drunk is what gets you sex. It might lower everyone's inhibitions and make them do things they'd think twice about if they were sober, but having sex with some girl who wakes up the next day and really wishes she hadn't slept with you, or else waking up yourself and feeling horribly embarrassed about what you did last night, isn't the best blueprint for a happy healthy sex life.

Drugs, apart from being illegal, do nothing for sex. Heroin can stop you getting a hard-on entirely, speed makes your willy shrink to the size of a petrified whelk, acid is too weird for sex, Ecstasy is often just a poor combination of acid and speed, dope makes you paranoid about everything and cocaine turns you into a totally unattractive gibbering monster.

Sex may be a bit scary, it may be a bit difficult at times, but when it's good, it's heart-stoppingly, gob-smackingly wonderful. It's such a shame to blur the ecstatic sensations of sex with a load of low-grade chemicals. The best sex is pure sex.

Premature ejaculation

Coming too quickly, or the fear of coming too quickly, has got to rank up high on the all-male Worry Top Ten. It's like the whole business of big dicks and little dicks; men have managed to persuade themselves that how you 'perform' sexually is really important to who you are and what calibre of man you make.

As usual, this sort of male logic is a load of rubbish. If you think about it, the concept of premature ejaculation or coming too quickly suggests that there is a right time and a wrong time to come. Which isn't strictly true. Men have decided that the right time to come is after or at the same time as their female partner comes. The reasoning behind this is the idea that a 'good lover' or a 'real man' can hold back his ejaculation until his lover has enjoyed the sex fully and had her own orgasm.

This sort of thinking suggests that all women want, or are even able, to come during penetrative sex (where the penis is inside the vagina), which definitely isn't true. Women are turned on and excited to the extent of orgasm by all sorts of different things, like clitoral stimulation, breast caressing, massage, etc., many of which might not involve the penis at all. So, the male coming quickly inside the vagina might not be an issue.

Still, what men have decided is that premature ejaculation, where the male shoots his load 'too soon', is practically a cardinal sin. Yet nearly every male who has had a few sexual encounters will know that sometimes it's impossible not to come quickly. Especially early on in your sexual adventures, you can get so worked up and excited that you come at the slightest contact between your todger and a beautiful girl.

Sometimes just a gentle hand laid in your lap can make you pop your cork. It happens. And it has to be said, in many situations, girls can find it immensely exciting that you have come so uncontrollably. When you think about it, it's really quite a compliment. It shows how powerfully attractive they are. And also, just because you come very quickly the first time, doesn't mean you won't be able to come again, maybe much slower, after you've given the tackle a little rest.

◆ My boyfriend was suffering from coming too quickly and he worried that he wasn't satisfying me. But the fact is that we love each other and both know that good sex takes time. All I can say is that I felt flattered I turned my boyfriend on so much. I think that it is awful that boys should feel this way about something that is a natural part of sexual exploration. I think relaxing and not worrying about climaxing is the best way to solve the problem.

Sue (17)

As usual, girls seem to be a couple of streets ahead of us men in the sensible-thinking department. But despite this, men continue to attach a great amount of shame and inferiority to coming quickly. The stupid thing is that every male knows that when you masturbate you don't always come in the same length of time. You could be hurrying desperately to have a quick crank before dashing off to school and ejaculate within less than a minute. Or else you could be having a leisurely Sunday afternoon hand-shandy with your warmest sexual fantasies which goes on for a full half-hour.

So it's the same with sex. You might find yourself coming quickly, especially in the early days, but as you get more relaxed things will slow down. Mostly it's just about getting used to your own body and getting used to intensely exciting sexual situations. Experience and practice give you an ability to control and pre-judge the moment of ejaculation which usually results in being able to stave it off, by stopping for a short while till the feelings pass or else by simply slowing down the movements.

Men and boys give themselves a very hard time about the time they take to come:

● I'm nineteen and I have a big problem. I'm going out with a sixteen-year-old girl and we are very serious about each other. But every time we make love I have a premature ejaculation. The longest our lovemaking has lasted is only a few minutes. It makes me feel really depressed and I think my girlfriend doesn't enjoy sex because of this. How can I control my orgasm, it's tearing me apart?

Matt

● When my girlfriend and I have sex, foreplay lasts quite a long time, then when we start intercourse I ejaculate within several seconds. We cannot carry on as I lose my erection. We both joke about it but it makes me feel inadequate.

Capital Radio fan

● I am a sixteen-year-old boy and I know I have a real bad problem as my girlfriend gets frustrated. The problem is I don't last very long into sex before I come. A few days ago we spent a day at my house and as soon as I put a condom on and put it inside her I came straight away. Other times on average I last about a minute. I have not spoken to anyone about it because it is so embarrassing. I don't want my relationship to split because I'm not good enough.

Anon

I am seventeen and I suffer from premature ejaculation. My problem is that as soon as I become slightly sexually active with a girl, I ejaculate. I'm sure you appreciate the embarrassment and the hampering effects it is having on my sex life. Is there something I can do or take to help me?

Concerned

There is no right or wrong time to come. Some men come in one minute, others can last fifty minutes. This doesn't mean the man who lasts the longest is the better lover. Sex isn't just about thrusting and pumping away for hours on end. It's about warmth and affection and sensuality. A lot of women would say that just being humped for ages at a stretch is not very sexy or satisfying at all. And the longer the period of time a man can penetrate a woman doesn't mean the greater the chance of her achieving an orgasm. Penetration is not the only key to women's pleasure. Many prefer to be touched and stroked and caressed. They find these sensations more exciting.

In saying that, if a man finds he regularly comes more quickly than he and his partner want, then there *are* things he can do. There are even things they can do together to slow down the orgasm. One technique is to practise masturbating on your own to the point just before you come, then stop. Don't come. Wait for the come sensations to pass, then try again until you're about to come and then stop. Don't come. Keep doing this for four or five times. And practise this a few times a week. You can even do it with your partner where she masturbates you until you tell her to stop.

What this does is train you to control your orgasms so that you can recognize the feelings of when you are about to come and can stop in time. It takes practice, but usually it does make a difference.

Sex but *no* ejaculation

In the same way that many men get upset about coming 'too quickly', loads seem to suffer from exactly the opposite problem where they can't come at all.

● I had sex for the first time with my girlfriend and I really let her down as I didn't reach an orgasm. Is there something wrong with me? My friends all reach a climax. Ever since this we have been drifting apart. I really blame myself though I have tried to talk to her about it. It may be the end of our relationship but I still love her. Is it normal for a boy not to reach a climax?

Anxious (16)

● I am an eighteen-year-old boy. I have been going out with my girlfriend for eight months. We have made love several times. Although my girlfriend is very beautiful and I love her very much, I find that when we are making love, I cannot reach the point of ejaculation. We've found that when we are not making love I can ejaculate by other means. Have I got a major problem inside me? I am also so worried that I will never be able to start a family. I feel I am not worthy of her even though she tries to reassure me.

Worried video fan

Not being able to come during sex is a very common problem. Just like premature ejaculation, it often occurs early on in your sex life, or else at times when sex is a bit stressful. Having a new girlfriend could make you sexually nervous, which could easily inhibit you and stop you ejaculating. Nerves have a very powerful effect on erections and ejaculation. We should never underestimate how much of the sex goes on inside our heads. We can blame various parts of our body, well, *one* in particular usually, but the problem is often inside our head. When we get nervous and worked up about sex, the strain shows down below.

Men and boys can get weird about sex. We take so much on board and give ourselves such a hard time about performing well. Then we assassinate ourselves when we think we're 'bad' at sex. We assume that we have failed as men if we've 'failed' at sex. What a lot of tosh!

The less performance obsessed we can be about sex, the more we can enjoy it and the more real contact and real communication we can have with our partners. If a guy is so intent on lasting twenty-five minutes during penetrative sex, the chances are all his efforts are being concentrated into his dick, keeping it from coming. But if you think about it, this is actually quite off-putting for the woman.

A lot of women complain that a man seems distant and distracted during sex, which is not very flattering or loving for them. This is often because he's concentrating so hard on not coming. It's no great turn-on for her. He's giving himself a hard time and the sex suffers as a result.

It would make much more sense and be much more sexy if there was more communication, more fun and less worry.

Orgasms

To be absolutely blunt, too much fuss is made about orgasms.

Women have historically had a raw deal on the orgasm front. It used to be that women's needs and desires weren't considered during sex. Men would just do their bit, have a hump and then come. If the women got anything out of it, well good for them. But there was never any pressure put on men to help their partners enjoy sex. Traditionally women were meant to 'lie back and think of England'.

Most thoughtful male lovers these days would think it pointless and unsatisfying to have sex if their partner's feelings and desires weren't taken into consideration. The idea of having sex with a woman and not caring if she's enjoying it is well out of order. You might as well be having sex with a prostitute, where her only interest is the money.

But, in saying that, orgasms are only one aspect of good sex. They're not the be-all and end-all: you don't have to come to have a seriously exciting sexual experience.

Indeed, the quest for the orgasm can get a bit tedious for both men and women. Too much fuss is made about orgasms in books and magazines and films. A lot of people, both men and women, get to feel inadequate about sex if they and their partner aren't coming with great earth-shattering squeals every five minutes. This sort of sex only really exists in the fantasy of Hollywood movies.

Male orgasms are a bit hard to define. Some would say that if you've come, then you've had an orgasm. But that's not strictly true. You can ejaculate and feel very little. Other times you can ejaculate, usually during good sex, and it feels like your whole body has been turned inside out.

Orgasms shouldn't be seen as the ultimate goal of sex. If you just view orgasms as the real goal of sex then you can easily end up disappointed. To be too obsessed by orgasms is narrow minded. There's a lot more to sex than coming.

Orgasms can be a let down. Apart from anything else, when you come, it usually means the end, or the start of the end of your lovemaking. If you don't come, you can go on doing different things as long as you both enjoy it.

Some people find orgasms a bit scary. The sensations of intense pleasure and of being out of control for a moment can have the effect of making some people feel down and vulnerable.

So much of the stuff written and said about sex deals with great earth-shattering heights of pleasure that come from orgasm. This is fantasy sex. A lot of times sex is just a comfy, caring, quite pleasurable thing two people who love each other do. It can sometimes be great. It's often just OK. It can also be bad. To get too sensation-seeking about sex will lead to disappointment.

The best thing about sex is not what happens, and what you did, it's who you did it with, what you both felt about it and about each other. Sex is not very often a huge, breathtaking, ground-breaking event. Most of the time it's just a small, warm, comfy-feeling thing.

Feeling *iffy* without a *stiffy*

Next to coming too quickly, the biggest other problem that men have is that they lose their erections before or during sex. Again this is one of those problems which men feel so embarrassed and shameful about that they never discuss it with each other. They're too shy to admit it because they think that their mates will just laugh and take the mickey. The sad thing is that this is probably true.

All the same, problems with erections that won't go up or stay up are very, very common:

⚫ I've started going out with a girl who has a reputation for going out with boys. The problem is I can't get an erection when we start to play with each other. All she can say is, 'The other lads got one, why don't you? Don't you love me?' I'm still a virgin at eighteen. Is this a serious problem? I even think of turning gay.

Joe

⚫ I have been going out with this girl I love for two years. Recently we tried having sex. I brought condoms and was very careful, but my penis wouldn't stiffen up. I am so embarrassed. She was understanding but I knew she was disappointed. Is there something wrong with me?

Distressed (16)

⚫ I am twenty years old and have been going out with my girlfriend for nearly a year. I'm getting really frustrated because every

time we go to make love I have an erection
at first, but when we actually go to do it, the
erection goes off. My girlfriend keeps thinking
it's because I don't love her. I do. I just can't
get it to stay hard.

Tom

● I am seventeen years old. Recently, after
discussing it, my girlfriend and I decided to
have sex, which was a new experience for both
of us. We took all the precautions and once I
had an erection I went to put on a condom,
but then found I wasn't erect any more.
Because of this we couldn't have sex properly.
I have tried since but the same thing
happened. What is wrong with me? Why can't
I put a condom on and stay erect? I feel a
failure.

Anon

● I'm seventeen and when my girlfriend and
I try to make love I can never get an
erection even though I'm quite excited. I can
get an erection before, but when I put my
penis into her I just flop. I have only known
my girlfriend for a short while and I think this
will put her off me. Even though she seems
to be very understanding she says that it
might have something to do with drink. Could
this have something to do with it?

Embarrassed from Leeds

● I have had sexual relationships before with
girls and I could come with them. With
them I would go hard and have an orgasm but
with my new girlfriend I can't even get a hard-

on. I am afraid of sex with this girl. I think that
if I try to have sex with her I won't come and
it would be so embarrassing. I really love her
very deeply. This is the best relationship I have
ever had with a girl. I am afraid that I will lose
her.

Worried

The willy is an unreliable tool. It's sensitive to stress
and often acts in an unpredictable manner. Most men
have experienced loss of erection at exactly the
moment they would least expect it to happen. Even
when they feel very excited and absolutely raring to
go, suddenly the willy can shut down all systems and
turn back into the warm soft sleepy thing it so often
likes to be.

Drink can make it go floppy. So can fitting a
condom. Having sex with the most beautiful girl in
the world can make it go floppy. Having sex for the
first time with a girl, or someone you really love, or
having sex somewhere strange or stressful, expecting
your parents to appear home suddenly from the
bingo, or doing it in the back of the car, all these
things can have a counteractive effect on the todger.

Even nothing in particular or specific can make it
go soft. One night out of the blue, for no apparent
reason, your dick could suddenly decide that it's not
going to stay hard or even go hard in the first place.
Be warned, this does happen and it's perfectly and
absolutely, dead-boringly normal.

So, you might lose your erection. So what? There's
nothing you can do except forget about it, get on
with some warm kissing and cuddling and try again
later. Don't try to hide it or get angry or blame your
girlfriend. It's far better and far more useful just to
have a laugh at the unpredictability of your willy and

get on with something else. If you turn it into a big deal you're more likely to upset your partner and yourself and stop yourself from getting hard later.

The more pressure you put yourself under and the more of an issue you turn it into, the more difficult it becomes to function.

Don't ever kid yourself that you're master of the monster that lives inside your Y-fronts. You're not. It'll trip you up (not literally), fool you and fox you, trick you and tease you, embarrass you and abandon you a lot of times, all through your life.

There's nothing you can do about it, except accept it. And be reassured in the simple knowledge that even though they never seem to admit it openly, every other male is experiencing exactly the same stuff too, time and time again.

Sex & your Sausage

A *price*less organ

There's no doubt about it, the willy is a fabulous organ. It may not be the most complicated or sophisticated of our organs but it certainly delivers a lot more fun than some of them. In all my life I can't remember having one good experience from my liver, or my kidneys come to that. But the little one-eyed trouser snake has given me a whole heap of dreamy feelings, heart-stopping moments and even quite a few laughs.

No matter how brilliant we think our knobs are, there is no excuse for using them instead of a brain. Too many males rely on their tackle to make major life decisions, and this can be a big mistake.

Sex is a very powerful thing. Even after thousands of years of Man's evolution, we are still easily enslaved to something as basic as sex. You only have to look at advertising trends to see that we haven't come very far since the cave-dwelling days!

If a manufacturer wants to sell a new model of motor, what do they do? They get a bunch of top-class supermodels to stand around in various states of provocative undress caressing the aforementioned set of wheels and we very quickly take notice. It doesn't mean we all rush out and empty our building society books to buy one. But we sure notice the adverts.

Because sex is so powerful, men and women often make errors of judgment: they're more influenced by their hormones than by their sense of decency, fair play or conscience.

People start affairs, have sex before they're ready, have sex with obviously wrong partners, have sex without contraception or precaution and then end up feeling terrible. An awful lot of people have experienced sex that they regret.

First-time sex

It's very hard, especially in your teens when your hormones are tugging you up and down like a yo-yo, to imagine that some sex can be unpleasant or wrong. When your tackle is screaming out to be used, it's easy to think that any sex is good sex. This isn't true. Some sex is awful. First-time sex for a lot of people is a major disappointment.

One of the reasons why first-time sex is often so unfulfilling is because people rush into doing it.

1 They don't know the person they're having it with well enough.

2 They aren't relaxed enough.

3 They choose to do it somewhere inappropriate or uncomfortable.

4 They don't have enough time.

5 They don't know what they're doing.

6 They haven't got adequate contraception.

7 Basically, they just aren't ready for sex.

And it's such a pity to rush it because a lot of boys only end up thinking they're inferior and inadequate, and girls think they've done something wrong. Or didn't do something they should have.

For boys, one of the major problems is being a virgin. Male teenage peer pressure makes it very difficult to be a virgin. Boys take the mickey out of each other if they haven't had sexual experiences by the age of fifteen or so. They often start publicly ridiculing the boys who haven't started or managed to score in the sexual exploration field. And so, as a boy you can be forced into making the choice of either lying about your sexual adventures, which many decide is the easiest option, or else you have experiences with girls you maybe don't even like and definitely aren't ready for.

Being a virgin is made very hard for some boys, not only by other boys, but even by some girls too:

I am seventeen and still a virgin. My girlfriend keeps pressing me to have sex. But I am too embarrassed because I am not very well developed and don't know much about sex. I am just scared that she will laugh at me and then dump me. Our relationship is very close at the moment and I feel if I don't have sex with her soon it will fail.

Andy

I am a seventeen-year-old virgin male. I've been seeing a girl of the same age for a fortnight and she was all too keen to have sex. At the crucial moment my nerves got the better of me and I stupidly said, 'What do I do next?' My girlfriend finished with me like a shot and I was left the butt of all jokes at college. Apart from the embarrassment of this, my confidence and self-esteem have been shattered. I'm afraid I'll never have the bottle to approach another woman.

Anon

● I am a fifteen-year-old boy and I have a big problem. You see, all of my friends have lost their virginity and brag about how good it was. I am the only one who has not had sex yet. I really want to impress them. The main problem is that I am ugly and I have no girlfriend. Once or twice I have considered prostitution but I know this is a dirty thing to do. But how can I get the girls to like and have sex with me before my friends find out I'm a virgin?

Anxious

In some boys' minds sex becomes this sort of abstract thing that is connected to relationships or love. It's just something you have to do in order to earn your place amongst your peer group. Apart from anything else, this suggests that the quality of the sex, and the quality of any emotion that goes on between the two people having sex, are not as important as the impressed reaction of your mates. If you're only having sex to impress your mates, then is it any wonder so many girls feel they get a raw deal?

A lot of girls have sex with the wrong boy or have sex before they feel ready and soon wish they hadn't:

◆ I feel cheap and nasty because of something that recently happened to me. We went clubbing and after a drink I ended up going back to this lad's house with my

friend. I ended up having sex with this guy who
I had never met before. I wanted to wait until
I'd found the right person as I was a virgin. I
feel I have betrayed myself.

Distressed (17)

◆ I was going out with this boy for just over
a month. He was really popular at school
and it was a dream come true that he was
actually mine. At the time the main topic at
school was sex. Almost all my friends were
speaking of their experiences and I had
nothing to say. I felt I was being left behind. I
knew he wouldn't say no because he was
quite experienced, so I made a move and we
ended up having sex. My first time was not
one to remember. For the first few days I was
glad I had something to say when the topic
was brought up, but soon I began to regret it.
We broke up not long after. I discovered
having sex doesn't mean you're grown up.

Lucy (15)

One of the cruel ironies of life and society is that boys
think they are more attractive and acceptable to girls
if they have lost their virginity. But many girls feel
ashamed if they have had sexual experience:

◆ I am eighteen and have had two sexual
relationships. One with a boy I was going
with for eighteen months, the other with
someone I used to see from time to time. Now
I have met someone who I think is a virgin. I
like him a lot, but my problem is that I'm
racked with guilt. I'm too scared of getting
involved in another relationship because aside

from possibly making another mistake, I'll have
to explain my past. If a girl explained this to
you, would you think her a slag?

Deborah

There's a misplaced belief amongst some males that
being a bit of a lad and having sown your wild oats
makes you a thoroughly lived-in man of the world.

Strangely enough, most women don't actually see
the practice of bonking-anything-with-a-pulse as an
attractive element of a man's character. But a lot of
boys think this is what you're supposed to do. They
get dragged into another one of those male-
generated myths about being a stud. Lads think they'll
appear more impressive to their mates if they're seen
to be putting it about. Trouble is, they worry too much
about their mates' reactions and don't even consider
the females' point of view.

Some boys seriously think that by having had some
sexual experiences it will make them attractive to girls.
They firmly believe that being a virgin means no girl
will want to go out with them and definitely won't
have sex with them.

A lot of girls who've written to me say exactly the
opposite. Not only are girls *not* put off by boys being
virgins, they actively prefer virgin boyfriends:

◆ I would definitely prefer to lose my
virginity to a boy who was a virgin. Even
if I was experienced, I'd be perfectly happy to
have sex with a boy who was still a virgin. I
consider them a great turn-on!

Vicky (15)

◆ I think being a virgin is a really attractive
quality in a boy. I hate boys who go

around bragging about how many girls they've slept with. They are a real turn-off. Being a virgin shows that he is a caring and mature guy who hasn't just slept with every girl he's been out with.

Dee (16)

◆ I would love to go to bed with a virgin. I lost my virginity when I was fourteen. The guy I lost it to wasn't a virgin and I felt very uncomfortable. It was a total nonevent and I thought I hadn't done something right. We hate each other now and I wish I was a virgin so I could lose my virginity to someone who loved me and was also a virgin.

Kelly (16)

◆ I find it a real turn-off if a boy's had sex before, because I feel intimidated by his experience. If ever I went to bed with a male who wasn't a virgin I'd be embarrassed because he'd expect me to know what to do as well.

Anon (14)

So, a lot of boys lie about their experiences or have experiences that they don't enjoy any more than the girls do in order to brag to their mates and raise their status as non-virgins. But the truth of the matter is that if they could just admit to being inexperienced and virgins, then a whole lot of girls would probably find them more attractive and easier to go out with.

It all comes back to that business of being more concerned about what your mates think of you than what the sex itself is like or what girls feel about the whole deal.

Having sex for the sake of sex is often a very empty and unfulfilling experience, but having sex simply for the sake of your reputation among your mates is just very, very sad.

Sex *without* the sausage

When you think about it, the idea of virginity and experience is a very weird business. Technically speaking you are no longer a virgin when you have finally played hide the sausage with a girl. As soon as your penis has entered a girl's vagina, you are not a virgin.

But what is the big deal? The act of slipping a penis inside a vagina is not in itself any great wonder, especially as the chances are you'll come within seconds and the whole thing will be over before it's really started.

But all the same, as soon as the thing's in there, you're no longer a virgin. It's daft. To think that the very basic, minimal and often deeply unsatisfying event of this first entry can carry such weighty significance in the eyes of boys is laughable.

Most boys would actually become much better lovers and much more sensual men if they forgot about their dicks for a while when it comes to sex. An eagerness to plunge it into a vagina means that the whole event will soon be over, but it also misses so much other good stuff by being too focused on the penetration.

Sex that doesn't involve penetration can be stuff like mutual masturbation, where you both caress and stimulate each other's genitals by hand. Then there's oral sex; where you excite each other by licking or sucking each other's sex organs.

Then there's great stuff that doesn't involve the sex organs at all. Stuff like massaging each other's bodies, rubbing oil on every inch from top to toe in a warm candlelit room. Or playing striptease, watching each other slowly, slowly undressing and drinking in every tantalizing inch of exposed flesh.

All these sensual, sexy things take a little bit of imagination and effort, but they pay off big dividends. They can spice up and prolong your sex or they can be an alternative to always playing hide the sausage. There is an awful lot more to sex than what hangs between your legs.

Deep frenchie snogging

French kissing is one of the mysterious wonders of the world. We all grow up thinking it's some sort of really exotic, complicated and deeply naughty kissing ritual, which is about as close to sex as you can get without actually having it.

This, of course, is a load of rubbish. French kissing is simply about kissing with your mouth open wide enough to slide your wet pink tongue into the mouth of the person you're kissing. Or else to allow their tongue into yours.

People get hung up about French kissing. They think that it's so complicated that they won't be able to do it right and the world and their whippet will laugh at them for ever more. Thing is, French kissing is easy if you don't try too hard. If you thrust your tongue into someone's mouth and swirl it round like a demented cement mixer, it's not very pleasant for anyone concerned.

The best French kisses start very slow and

tentatively with your tongues just hardly touching but gradually getting slightly deeper into each other's mouths, only if both parties are keen. The worst thing in the world is being really deeply kissed when that's not what you want.

Some people don't like French kissing. It's not everyone's cup of tea by a long shot. A good kisser is not someone who can swish around with his tongue for hours on end. A good kisser is someone who can listen and feel what the person he's kissing likes. He's also someone who can talk to the person he's kissing before and after those kisses, making them all the more intimate and personal.

Good kissing's not about technique – it's about feeling. You can be kissed by the world's most practised kisser, but if you've got no feelings for them, it won't be half as good as a tiny peck from someone you adore.

Bragging

There are two main types of bragging. There's bragging about the size of your knob and bragging about what you've done with it.

Some boys love to give their todgers pet names. Stuff like Harry, Hercules, Big Boy, The Beast, Lollypop, Rocky and Giant Jake are pretty much par for the course.

I used to work in a pub with a guy who was always talking about his dick. It was really quite off-putting. He'd even talk about how big it was and what he liked to do with it and the things girls said when they saw it. I could never quite work out *why* he was telling me. Was it to impress me? To make me feel inferior?

I really don't know. He talked about it as though it were a person; sometimes called it his 'Little Brother' or his 'Old Man'.

The other common brag is when boys tell you in every intimate detail what they did with what girl, where and when. Again the suggestion is that you're supposed to be impressed, in awe of them and jealous that they have such good luck with the opposite sex.

But you can't help thinking, if they're having such a good time with all this, why do they have to tell me? It's as though they have to brag about it to make it seem good.

I know myself, I've been guilty of bragging about sex when I was younger, and I know I didn't tell the truth. Not only did I exaggerate some of the details; also made it out to be something really great, when in truth there were times I didn't think it was that great. But by lying I could almost persuade myself it was good and that it was worth doing.

Bragging can just become an elaborate way of lying to yourself about the disappointment you feel. If you can legitimize something by telling all your mates what a great time you had, then you don't have to feel bad about it. Yet we boys do this a lot of the time, we're not *honest* about how things really feel or really affect us. Instead we lie, not just to others but to ourselves. By lying we never have to face our real feelings, which means we never change the way we are. Which is a pity because then we just go on making the same mistakes and feeling worse and worse about it inside.

By putting a brave face on it we only cover up the truth. And the other damaging thing is that by lying to mates we encourage others to go off and do the same thing. And the lie continues. If they feel bad about it or don't have a good time, they think that there's something wrong with them. But instead of admitting their fears, they lie. And so it goes.

Bragging about sex, especially sex that was disappointing, is the start of a lie that can continue through a lifetime. And the sad part is that if you could admit there's maybe something wrong or something you're not sure about, there's a good chance you could get to the root of the problem and solve it. But if you just lie to cover it up, then you might be stuck with it for life.

Condoms

Considering that condoms were specifically designed for men to wear during sexual intercourse, we don't have a very good track record of using them. Sure, as lads we've always been very good at taking them into the toilets, turning them into water bombs and chasing first years round the playground with them. But using them for the purpose for which they were intended is another matter.

There are a lot of stupid male myths that make condoms seem uncool. Men claim that they ruin sex; that sex in condoms feels like 'taking a bath in your wellies' or 'eating a Mars bar with the wrapper on'. Some men claim that sex with condoms isn't as good as 'real sex'. Or even that sex with condoms is for kids and beginners, that real men don't use them. As usual this is all tripe of the first order.

The fact of the matter is that these days, with all the elaborate sexually transmitted diseases that are on offer, including HIV, it makes sense to wear a condom. And by wearing a condom you're not only showing sense and respect to your own todger, you're also showing that you care about the health of your partner.

Of course there are some guys who think that taking the risk of catching a disease or getting a girl pregnant all adds to the excitement of the sex. This is a bit like saying that driving a car with dodgy brakes makes your motoring more fulfilling.

Of course there may be times when using a condom does make you lose your erection. The business of faffing around getting one out of the packet might take the edge off your stiffy. But as we all know, stiffies are not all that hard to come by. With a little care and attention from you or your partner, your knob can soon be back to peak firmness.

And the opposite can also be said for condoms; they can sometimes improve and enhance your sex. For a start there's all that business of getting your partner to put the condom on for you. Many is the game that can be played out whilst putting on a johnny. Apart from anything else, it means that you'll get your willy touched and caressed in the process.

It's also a very good way for your partner to get to know your willy. Many girls never really get to touch and investigate the knob, because its owner is too shy or too eager to plunge it in. As we all know, willies may not be the prettiest creation in the universe, but they are damned interesting things to fiddle about with. Especially if you haven't got one of your own. It seems unfair to deprive your partner of the pleasure.

And the whole business of putting on a condom means that you have to stop or at least slow down the progress of your sexual exploration. This can often be a very useful little rest. If you don't stop, and just plough straight on, getting more and more excited with what you're doing, chances are you'll get too excited and come before you or your partner have had that much of a chance to enjoy the penetration.

But by stopping to put on a condom you may well find that you can actually gain better control of your orgasm. Condoms can definitely help delay you from coming so quickly.

It doesn't help that condoms are thought to be a bit tricky and technical to use (see page 99). There are a lot of different types of condom and they each come with instructions. This can scare a lot of boys. It's that same old problem that boys suffer from: they don't know something but feel they *ought* to know it, so they're too embarrassed to ask anyone, because then they'll look a fool, so instead they pretend they *do* know. Or else they go to elaborate lengths to avoid the thing that they don't know.

Basically, we are very scared of looking stupid or inexperienced, so we avoid doing things that are going to catch us out. A condom is one of those things:

> ● I am going out with a sixteen-year-old girl. I like her very much and don't want to lose her. She says she wants to go to bed with me. I wasn't sure so I suggested we wait. But I think she will finish with me if I don't make a move soon. I don't want to lose her because she's the best thing that's ever happened to me. But I have a problem, I don't know how to use a condom.
>
> *Anxious*

The range and variety of condoms on sale can be a minefield from the start. There are all these

different brands and types that are made for our con-
venience, but if we don't know what the difference
is, we're going to look daft. So, we're into scary terri-
tory from the off:

● Me and my girlfriend both feel we are
ready to have sex. But I want to know
which condoms are the best. I want to use
Durex, but there are five types. What are the
differences and which would protect me and
my girlfriend the best?

David

● I'm very worried. I love my girlfriend very
much and I am wondering which
condoms are the most protective and reliable
ones. I want this to be very special for my
girlfriend.

Leigh

● I've been going out with this girl for three
years. We have decided to have sex. Can
you tell me which condoms are the most
protective and how to go about having sex
with her. I really want it to be special.

Worried

● My girlfriend and I are thinking of having
sex for the first time and want to take
precautions, but we are not sure what to use.
What types of condoms are there, are there
different sizes, which are the most reliable and
safest condoms, which are the best makes?

Dale

Since HIV and AIDS came on the scene, condoms have become more and more important – not just as a means of contraception but also as protection. Although they aren't totally safe, using condoms makes sexual intercourse much safer and greatly reduces the risk of catching anything.

Their new-found importance has meant that condom manufacturers and marketing people have gone over the top trying to persuade the public to buy them. They've done this by making them more exotic and unusual. Which might make them more attractive on one level, but it also makes them more confusing on another. When there were just a couple of brands available, then you couldn't really go far wrong.

These days there are basically six different types of condom you can buy:

Allergy: ones like Durex Allergy which are specially designed for anyone who is allergic to the spermicide that they use in conventional condoms.

Flavoured: these come in all sorts of exotic flavours from chocolate mint to pina colada. They include ones like Durex Safe Play Minty and Jiffi Cocktail. The idea of the flavouring is to make them more fun and more tasty during oral sex.

Ribbed: brands like Durex Arouser and Mates Ribbed have rings of raised rubber ribs along their length in order to give an extra sensation inside the girl's vagina during sex.

Extra strong: Mates Super Strong are made thicker than other condoms for extra safety.

Extra thin: Brands like Durex Featherlite and Durex Elite are made thinner for extra sensitivity.

Extra big: There are a couple of brands like Le Condom Maxx and Magnum which are designed especially for boys who have ego problems and think they need bigger condoms.

One important rule to stick to when you're buying condoms is that you check that they've got the British Standards Kitemark printed on the packet. What this means is that they've been through rigorous safety checks. If you buy ones that don't have the Kitemark you don't know how dependable they're going to be.

Anyone who's ever been fishing probably knows the saying that 'most fishing tackle is designed to catch the fisherman, not the fish'. It's the same with condoms. You can fall into the trap of thinking that a coconut-flavoured, extra-ribbed, pink one with a tickling tip is going to make you the dog's bollocks when it comes to hot loving. Not true. A fancy condom does not a good lover make. Most of the time, it's best to keep things simple and concentrate on being kind, warm, loving and understanding.

A very small number of men find that they get a red itchy rash when they use condoms. This can obviously make it uncomfortable to wear them. What the makers of Durex suggest, if you do have any itchy redness when using condoms, is to swap to Durex Gossamer. Most Durex condoms and many other brands are lubricated with Nonoxynol 9, which is a spermicidal lubricant. Any allergic reactions tend to be to this chemical. Durex Gossamer use another lubricant called Sensitol. If after swapping to Gossamer the itchy rash doesn't go away, then try Durex Allergy, which doesn't have a spermicidal lubricant.

A very, very few men find they still have a bad reaction to Durex Allergy, which means that they are most likely allergic to the latex rubber which the condoms are made of. If that's the case, and it's a very rare condition, there are some condoms available made of animal gut that don't contain latex.

◆ My boyfriend won't wear condoms. He refuses to wear one because he says they are embarrassing. How can I get him to wear a condom and get over his embarrassment?

Dominique

◆ I am a troubled eighteen-year-old. I want to have sex with my boyfriend. He's the first boy I've ever been serious about and I'm afraid of losing him. I don't want to go on the Pill as it's bad for my health, but my boyfriend refuses to use condoms. He says that they're embarrassing to buy. What can I do to change this?

Sarah

Buying condoms can be a bit embarrassing because no matter what the person who is serving you *really* thinks, you can always imagine they're having a laugh or a scowl at what you might be about to do with these condoms. Buying them from teenage female shop assistants can be hard. There is no doubt about it – there's something very disquieting about buying condoms from someone you'd actually quite fancy using them with.

That's why vending machines in gents' toilets were invented. In pubs and clubs and some train stations you can serve yourself in the privacy of a public lavvy. In supermarkets you can get them and bury them in amongst a load of non-embarrassing gear. In petrol garages you can buy them off glassy-eyed cashiers who couldn't give a monkey's if you were the Pope. You can get them from mail order catalogues like Freemans (see p. 119 for address) and no one will ever be any the wiser.

Practise!

There is no point going to all the trouble of buying a condom and carrying it around for weeks, months and years, if, when it comes to the big moment, you can't get the thing to go on right. And let's face it, when you are about to have sex, maybe for the first time, chances are you'll be nervous, your hands will be shaking, heart pounding and mind on something much more engaging than what it says on the instructions inside the pack.

So the answer is, don't wait until the big moment before you fit a condom for the first time!

Practise at home. Take a few condoms into your bedroom and experiment with them. Try fitting one. Have a wank with one on. Try putting them on in the dark. Try fitting them with one hand. Try everything. The better you know your way around the condom, the more time you get to concentrate on and enjoy the sex you're about to have.

Remember, forewarned is forearmed and all that guff.

Getting round to *using* them

Even if you're one of those sensible lads who doesn't believe all the myth and tosh about condoms being bad news, it still doesn't mean you'll know how to use one. Every packet has a little sheet of instructions which it's obviously wise to follow carefully.

First make sure that the condom is the right way round. There's often a little teat at the top for catching the spunk, make sure this is sticking out. Squeeze it between your thumb and forefinger to make sure the air is expelled. And while squeezing, unroll the condom down the length of your penis, right to the base. If the condom is on inside out, you won't be able to unroll it all the way, and it certainly won't work.

After you've come, hold the condom in place round the base of your penis as you carefully withdraw from the vagina. This stops it slipping off or any spunk escaping down the side of the condom.

Condoms slipping off seem to be a regular worry:

● I use condoms with my girlfriend because I think they are the best contraception you can get and I don't want to get her pregnant. I've tried all different types of condoms but they keep falling off. I am a bit small, could this be the problem?

Don

● My problem is that all the girls that I've had serious relationships with have finished with me because my Durex keeps slipping off during intercourse. I can't understand why this happens because I follow all the directions on how to put them on. My last relationship fell apart because of this problem. What can I do to improve my love life?

Colin

Condoms don't just slip off of their own accord. Usually what happens is that your erection might dwindle a bit during sex. The trick is to keep checking that it's in place while you're making love just in case it slips and always make sure you withdraw as soon as you've come.

If a condom does slip off or if by any chance it splits during sex, don't keep quiet and pretend it hasn't happened. Be honest and own up because the risk is that the girl could get pregnant. If a condom has fallen off or split, she will have to go to the doctor or a Family Planning Clinic to get a Morning After Pill. This can be taken up to seventy-two hours after sex. This pill acts as a post-sex contraceptive and will stop her becoming pregnant. It is pretty unpleasant for the girl though – so don't regard this as an easy option. It's a contraceptive to be used only in an emergency.

Talking about condoms

Some men are scared of condoms, some are flummoxed by them and some aren't quite sure which ones to use. But nearly every man is shy of talking about condoms. There again, so are girls.

Thing is, you feel you can't get on to the subject if it's early in the relationship. Like you've just sat down for your first burger together and you launch into: 'Which d'you prefer, ribbed or flavoured?' It wouldn't work, would it? For a start it's presumptuous, you don't want to jump the gun and talk about sex when you're still nowhere near sure whether it's on the cards or not.

Also, a lot of blokes don't want to take any responsibility for contraception. They'll use it if they're asked to and if a condom is provided, but they think it's ultimately the girl's responsibility. If she wants to use one then she has to come up with the goods.

Not all men are like this. As we've seen from the letters, a lot of them are very concerned about keeping sex special and safe. That still doesn't mean they're quite ready to *talk* about condoms, sometimes they need encouragement. It might also help to know that girls have exactly the same worries:

◆ I don't want to catch AIDS or get pregnant, but I don't want to go on the Pill. So condoms seem like the only way out. I haven't asked my boyfriend about condoms, I haven't had the chance. It's not the type of thing that you'll talk about over the phone with your mum listening in. I really love him and want to have sex with him. I don't know how to bring up the subject of condoms. Do you have any ideas?

Sally

Talking about condoms isn't going to be easy. It's daft to pretend that there's any simple formula for getting into a sensible talk about condoms with your partner. The thing is not to leave it too late. Don't wait until you're both hot and excited in bed and there's no condoms within ten miles, because then you might just do it without and live to regret it.

If you think you might, possibly, maybe have sex,

then make sure some are handy. Don't try and talk about them in some really difficult situation which might be embarrassing, like on the bus or in front of her whole family at Sunday lunch.

There's no point in pretending that condoms fall naturally into conversations, they don't. They need to be introduced. Obviously the worry is that if you introduce them too early you might be seriously jumping the gun, making wild assumptions about what the next couple of hours might have in store, and so scare off the very person you're trying to get closer to.

But by talking about condoms before you get to the point of no return, you are showing a great respect for your partner and a real level of responsibility.

For boys who want to use condoms it's easier, they can simply put one on. For girls it's more difficult, they have to persuade the boy to wear one. The earlier this is tackled the better.

Look upon being able to talk about sex and condoms as a good indication of how well you know each other and how comfortable you are together. If you can't talk about sex or mention condoms, then the chances are you aren't really ready to be having sex together.

Oral sex

In my problem page postbags, oral sex is big news. You can guarantee every week there'll be a collection of letters on the subject. And nearly every single one of those are from *girls*. Most of the time the letters want to know what a blow job is and how to give one.

A blow job is simply when a willy gets sucked, licked and kissed. In the process of all this oral attention, the owner of the willy might experience an orgasm and come, or else he might just get to feel all manner of delicious sensations. Or he might not even like it.

There's no doubt, blow jobs can be a lot of fun. Having your dick sucked can be a most enjoyable and erotic experience. But it's not the be-all and end-all of life itself.

The thing is, blow jobs are a bit weird, a bit different and a bit sexually sophisticated. They require a bit more devotion and effort on the part of the giver than say a quick hand-job does, and they have a certain different feel from sex. There's no getting away from it, the sensations of having a soft warm mouth wrapped around your willy can be very nice. Although teeth and dental braces can sometimes be an uncomfortable extra.

Nice or not, let's not turn this simple physical sexual act into a religion. Part of the pleasure of being given oral sex is the comfort and knowledge that the person doing it *wants* to. Much as we males love and cherish our todgers, usually the thought of putting it in our mouths is not something we'd go a real bundle on. So partly it's the surprise and excitement that a girl should be so willing that has a real effect.

Blow jobs are different from sex as well because they are a passive act. You just have to lie or stand while it's done *to* you, rather than it being something you're doing to or with your partner.

It has to be said that blow jobs are often not that effective. Many males find it a lot harder to come from being sucked than they do from being tossed off or having sex, because the actual physical pressure just isn't the same. Blow jobs are often better when used as part of the overall foreplay rather than having to star as the main event. Too much concentration on the blow job can lead to a lost erection and a very stiff jaw.

The worst thing about blow jobs is that they've become this big-deal part of teenage sex. So many boys seem to have got it into their heads that they haven't really lived until they've had their willy in some girl's mouth. And as a result, some boys put pressure on girls to give them blow jobs.

What could be worse than sucking someone's penis when you don't really want to or aren't sure what to do? It's *definitely* something that should never be forced or pressured.

In saying that, most of the letters I get are from girls who *do* want to give blow jobs but don't know how:

◆ I've been going out with this lad for quite a while now and I'm really in love with him. I would do anything for him. The other day he asked me to give him a blow job. I told him maybe the next time, but the problem is I don't really know what it means.

Kim (16)

◆ We are two fifteen-year-old girls who have older boyfriends. The problem is that we would like to go further than kissing but we don't know much about sex. The two of us would like to know what a blow job is and how to do it, because we don't want to feel like silly little girls.

Louise and Karen

◆ I am seventeen and my boyfriend is
eighteen. He recently asked me to give
him a blow job. I have made excuses as to why
I don't give him them, but the real reason is
that I don't know how to. I don't know how
long I can come up with different excuses. My
boyfriend is beginning to think that I don't love
him. But I do very much and I want to make
him happy.

Depressed

In nearly all the letters I get, the idea of oral sex has
been raised by the boys. Girls do seem to want to
comply and show willing, but they aren't the ones
that started the ball rolling. Not surprisingly I've had
very few letters from boys whose girlfriends want the
boys to give them oral sex. There's definitely something about being given oral sex that appeals strongly
to the male of the species.

Giving a boy a blow job shouldn't be seen as some
sort of test of love and devotion. Some boys seem to
emotionally blackmail girls into giving them oral sex
as a way of proving their love. This is all wrong. Any
sort of sex that has to be forced or contrived is bad.

No one should feel obliged or pressured into having
any sort of sex before they decide they want to. That's
not what sex is about. Sex is about progressing and
developing at your own natural pace and doing things
because you and the person you're doing them with
enjoy it. Not because everyone else in your class says
they've done that already.

And blow jobs are not by any means an essential
part of sex. A lot of people don't like giving them or
even being given them. Some guys find it very hard
to come. Some feel dead embarrassed having their
lover's head bobbing around between their knees.

Just because blow jobs sound exotic and a bit naughty doesn't mean they're crucial.

There is a worry that blow jobs become too much the currency of teenage sex. It's like, boys want blow jobs so they pressurize girls into giving them. And girls then see blow jobs as a 'hurdle' of their teens, like losing their virginity. Girls can get very competitive about sexual experience with each other in the same way as boys.

Many girls end up losing their virginity or giving some boy a blow job, not because they particularly want to, but because they want to impress or keep up with their mates.

If blow jobs happen naturally as part of the sexual exploration and enjoyment that you have with your partner, then they can be a whole heap of fun. But if they have to be forced, they are not worth having.

Any Other Business

6

Testicles

I f you thought your knob was a weird-looking thing – what about your balls?! Maybe I'm biased, but I've always thought that women's bodies are things of great beauty. Even their sex organs are visually stimulating. Breasts are gorgeous, rounded sensual delights. And the sight of a smooth stomach arcing down to a triangle of fine pubic hair is a groin-stirring vision. But a pair of knackers? I don't think so.

They're a strange invention. They're housed in your scrotal sac which has a different-coloured skin from the rest of your body. A reddish pink if you've got white skin and a dark purple if you've got black. The skin tone actually changes during puberty as your testicles start to get bigger. The skin that surrounds them gets baggier and more wrinkly and usually each bollock hangs at a different height.

In most adult men the left testicle is lower than the right one. The reason for this is so that when you're running they don't crush together, one can comfortably sit just above the other.

The scrotum (which is the 'sac' of skin which holds the testicles beneath the penis) is where the sperm are made and stored ready for ejaculation. Sperm are very iffy about temperature, and actually like the climate to be a little lower than body temperature. That's why the balls dangle down away from the body, to keep them cool. And that's why wearing tight, constricting underwear is not good for your fertility: basically, you're overheating your sperm.

It's the same in reverse, when you climb out of a freezing swimming pool and your knackers are bunched up like two walnuts in a prune skin. They do that because they're trying to keep up there, as close to your body as they can, to grab a little heat.

Bollocks seem badly designed. There you are, carrying the future of your race, all your stored-up seed, in a puny little sac dangled daftly between your legs. Meanwhile your brain – a clever organ, though not quite clever enough to reproduce – is housed in a case of bone tougher than concrete!

Because of the precarious positioning of the testes, it's important to take care of them whilst doing dangerous things like hockey, cricket, boxing or karate. A box or cup protector should be worn at all times of sporting danger, to keep things sweet.

Losing a testicle is not the end of the world. Men who've lost one either through accident or disease can normally still have children. It seems we got given a pair just in case we lost one.

Will you *look* at those *bollocks!*

One of the things most schoolboys do at some time or other is kick each other in the nuts. It's hard to say exactly why, it's just another one of those bizarre male rituals we get so attached to. There's hardly a second year lad in the land who hasn't felt the boot or knee of some over-active, hormonally fuelled fourth former in his delicate knackers.

And does it hurt?! Does Kylie have a sister! There's no feeling like it in the whole world. The front of your face goes fuzzy, your balls go numb and then this dark evil ache starts in the very pit of your privates and oozes like lava up over your body, engulfing you in a sick-making, throat-bulging nausea.

In my school, older boys used to think it was great sport to walk up to a lad a couple of years younger and flick him in the cods with the back of their hand, shouting 'Cough!' at the same time. Needless to say, I did my fair share of writhing around the playground yeouwling like a cat on a hot tin roof, while cradling and comforting my aching goolies.

It's not surprising then that we aren't in a great hurry to fiddle around with our nuts at a later date. Most of the sensations associated with testicles are uncomfortable ones. Balls are round sensitive objects that curl up and die in the cold or else dangle and flop in the warm. Apart from that we don't take a whole lot of notice.

But, on the subject of doctors and health, bollocks are important. Testicular cancer is one of the most common forms of cancer to affect young men: nearly a thousand new cases are diagnosed every year. It's a cancer of the sperm-forming cells and young men are most vulnerable to it because it gets a grip when the hormones are working flat out producing sperm.

The good news is that it's a comparatively easy cancer to treat and *can* be cured. The thing is to detect it early. This is why we have to overcome any testicle trepidations and have a good old gander at those bollocks.

Genital health, or learning to look after your tackle,

must include an easy and regular relationship with your doctor, but it also takes a certain amount of vigilance on your own part. It's a bit like taking a peek under the bonnet of your car before you go on a long journey and checking you've got enough oil and no unpleasant knocking noises. So it's the same with your string and nugget set.

The first sign of trouble in testicles is usually a swelling in one ball and maybe a dull ache in the lower stomach or in the bollock itself. In order to keep aware of what's going on down below, it's important to have a proper peek yourself.

Just after you've had a hot bath, stand in front of a mirror and cup your cods in the palm of your hand. One ball is often a bit larger than the other, which is perfectly normal. What isn't normal are any lumps or bumps on the curving front or underside surface of the testicle. There is a thing at the top and the back of the bollock called the epididymus, which is a sort of squiggly lumpy structure where the sperm are stored and ripen. This is meant to be there. But any pea-shaped lumps you can feel sticking up on the rest of the ball are not meant to be there. If there's anything strange and out of place, then don't panic, just go and tell your doctor.

Doing a testicular examination once a month is an easy and sensible way to look after your tackle and keep ahead of any possible problems.

Foreskin hygiene is very important as well. Washing properly under and around your foreskin twice a day can ward off bacterial infection and possibly even help guard against penile cancer. Keep it clean and tidy, and not only is it going to be nicer to use and more pleasant for anyone else to handle, it'll also last you a lot longer too.

Although a lot of males get totally obsessed by the

size and shape of their tackle, there's an awful lot who don't do anything to look after it. Rather than just regarding it as something useful to pee through, fun to play with and ever-ready for the occasional spot of love-action, it makes much more sense to treat it as a constant companion.

Instead of always having a job for it to do every time you take it out of the garage, it's nice, once in a while, to wheel it out purely for a bit of tender loving care and attention.

We expect a lot from our three-piece set, so it's only fair to put a bit of care and maintenance back into keeping it sweet.

Getting it *caught* in things

The most common things to get your knob caught in are zips, photographs and girls.

There are boys who are clumsy with all of these things. Me, I was an early casualty of the zip trap. One summer I was playing football in the garden with my mates. I rushed indoors to have a wee, but was keen to get back outside quick because I was on to a possible hat trick. So I gave the winkle a quick shake, popped it back in my khaki shorts and whipped the zip up with one hand while the other was already on the door knob. Suddenly, I was overcome with this terrible pain.

It was like someone had squeezed a thousand lemons, mixed them with a gallon of onion vinegar, scrubbed my face with a Brillo pad and dunked me into the brew. Every inch of my existence stung. A trillion stinging nettles called out my name. I could hear tight-stretched violin strings screeching in my ears.

I looked down, and there it was, the sad little chipolata chomped between hard-edged, shiny steel zip-teeth that seemed to scoff at the tenderness of my most intimate flesh.

I was paralysed. I couldn't move forwards or backwards. Breathing was painful. My hands only fluttered like sparrows round a bird table, never daring to alight on the trousers, for fear of inducing more of the searing pain that washed in great crashing waves over my body.

At the very tender age of five, I had stood on the precipice of Hell and looked down into the writhing pit of agony. It brings tears to my eyes even now to think back to that raw and torturous moment in my formative years.

Thankfully, my dad came to the rescue on hearing my choked squeals and administered a steady hand and a tube of Savlon. I lived to tell the tale. I took great care with zips from that day forth. And I never, ever, got anywhere near scoring a hat trick at football again. Possibly, a world-class player was nipped in the bud.

Most men are a little shy and embarrassed about their penises. Unless they are very confident and show-offy, most of us like to keep it covered. Even in sexy situations, there is a tendency to slip under the covers and wriggle out of your boxers rather than be brash about it.

There are others though, the ones who are desperately proud of how well hung they are, who like to parade around at any opportunity making sure the assembled company clocks the size of their todger. Usually, this only ever happens in the changing room, where it's only other men who have to suffer the sight.

But there are some men who get sexually aroused by exposing themselves to women. 'Flashers' are often men who get a kick out of showing their dick to some female stranger. This sorry thrill usually comes about because they are unable to form proper relationships with women. They are sad cases who derive pleasure from sexual shocking. Often they are impotent men who are unable even to get an erection when it comes to close contact.

Flashing, or exhibitionism, is a criminal offence which can carry a sentence of imprisonment for up to twelve months. The traditional haunt of flashers is parks, where they get a kick out of showing their tool to some unsuspecting passing female. Obviously, this can be a very upsetting and frightening experience for any girl, although most of the time these sort of exhibitionists intend no real harm and don't want to touch or approach the person they're exposing themselves to. They are sick and sad men.

There's another sort of exhibitionism that goes on these days that is in some ways even more sick and sad. There's a type of lad who gets a big thrill out of getting drunk and taking his kit off to expose himself to the pub, club or coach.

And then there's the guys who have taken up the Michael Jackson habit of grabbing and tugging their crotch to emphasize a point or expression.

This recent trend in willy clutching and flashing is sad because it's also about a total inability to relate. Instead of being able to enter into a friendship and relationship that develops into sex, some boys can only short cut to communicating with their willy. And it's not as though it's a prelude to sex, because for most of these lads who're whipping off their trousers down the Rugby club in front of their mates and a few girls, it's *instead* of sex. They don't ever get past waving their dick about because they don't know how to communicate properly with girls.

Living with your Willy

The willy can be a man's best friend; bring him endless fun, excitement and comfort. But it can also be his worst enemy. There are men who think with their willy all their lives and end up sad, lonely old men.

Most men's knobs are attracted to sex and sexy things, but this attraction doesn't equal a relationship. Some men have sexual partner after sexual partner, and as each one loses her allure they move on to the next. So all that ever exists between them is sex.

Sex is good at times, and very good occasionally, but its appeal doesn't last for ever. What *can* last for ever is friendship. Although your willy might lead you glans-first into sexy situations and compel you towards attractive girls, what is important is that you also form relationships.

Your willy is not the best judge of character – you are.

Don't let it rule your life: it's a useful and fun accessory. Look after it and it will look after you. By all means listen to it when it's not feeling well and get it checked out quick, but remember that there are also times to ignore it.

Your brain is your biggest and best sex organ. It's inside there that you'll find sensible answers to life's questions, not inside your boxers.

The secret to a well willy is a well head.

Useful Addresses

Brook Advisory Centres
Telephone: **Freephone 0800 0185 023**
Phone for details of your nearest clinic.
Website: www.brook.org.uk

Family Planning Association
2-12 Pentonville Road
London N1 9FP
Telephone: **0845 122 8690**
Website: www.fpa.org.uk

GUM (Genito Urinary Medicine) Clinics
There are clinics at your local hospital or
call NHS Direct for details
Telephone: **0845 4647**
Website: www.homehealth-uk.com/medical/gumclinics.htm

National AIDS Helpline
Telephone: **Freephone 0800 567 123**
Website: www.fpa.org.uk

Terence Higgins Trust
52-54 Gray's Inn Road
London WC1X 8JU
Telephone: **Helpline 0845 1221 200**
Website: www.tht.org.uk